S0-AAB-600

HOW TO BE A
DURABLE HUMAN

ALSO BY JENIFER JOY MADDEN
The Durable Human Manifesto:
Practical Wisdom for Living and Parenting in the Digital World

Praise for *The Durable Human Manifesto*

"Beautiful and brilliant."
—ANNA WHISTON-DONALDSON, author of the New York Times
bestseller, *Rare Bird*

"Put down the laptop, stop checking your phone for emails, realize
that that Facebook upload can wait, and read this book."
—TERRY IRVING, author, publisher, former ABC News, MSNBC, and
CNN producer

"The word resilience is in—especially considering climate change. But
I've never been drawn to that word. It suggests a life of being knocked
down and standing up again and again (and it doesn't suggest a picture
of progress, but of survival). I like the word durable better. It's not a
're' word.
—RICHARD LOUV, author of *Last Child in the Woods: Saving Our Children
from Nature Deficit Disorder*

"This thin but powerful booklet can be read in five minutes, but the
ideas expressed could change your life."
—JOHN SHREFFLER, electronics manufacturer

published by

Austral Arc

HOW TO BE A
DURABLE
HUMAN

REVIVE AND THRIVE IN THE DIGITAL AGE
Through the Power of Self-Design

JENIFER JOY MADDEN

Austral Arc

Published by Austral Arc, LLC
© 2016 by Jenifer Joy Madden
All rights reserved

ISBN 987-0-9912426-3-4
First edition: May 2016
Printed in the United States of America

Cover design by Patty Wallace, MonkeyPAWCreative.com
Book design and illustrations by Marisa Fritz

No part of this publication may be reproduced or transmitted in any form or by any means, including informational storage and retrieval systems, without permission in writing from the copyright holder, except for brief quotations used with attribution.

This publication is solely for informational purposes and not intended to provide medical advice. Neither the author nor publisher take responsibility for any possible consequences from any treatment, procedure, exercise, dietary modification, action or application of medication which results from reading or following the information contained in this publication. The reader should consult a physician in matters relating to his or her health, particularly for symptoms that may require diagnosis or medical attention.

Although the author and publisher have made every effort to ensure that the information in this publication was correct at the time of publication, the author and publisher do not assume, and hereby disclaim, any liability to any party for any loss, damage, or disruption caused by errors or omissions, whether such errors or omissions result from negligence, accident, or any other cause.

Address inquiries to info@australarc.com.

www.AustralArc.com

For my father, Charles Alexander Joy, M.D.,
who taught me to love and respect the human condition

CONTENTS

It's Time to Be Durable...1

Chapter 1: Design Your Self 9

Chapter 2: Activate.. 19

Chapter 3: Choose Your Place............................... 29

Chapter 4: Respect Your Structure 41

Chapter 5: Pay Attention...................................... 53

Chapter 6: Seek Sleep and Sanctuary...................... 67

Chapter 7: Come to Your Senses 77

Chapter 8: Manage Your Mind.............................. 99

Chapter 9: Embrace Your Nature...........................117

Thank You...123

Acknowledgments...125

Notes...127

IT'S TIME TO BE DURABLE

The pessimist complains about the wind; the optimist expects it to change; the realist adjusts the sails.

William Arthur Ward, author of *For This One Hour*

Not long ago, we humans were at the top of our game. Guided by the sun and the stars, we traveled the globe, propelled by curiosity to ingeniously solve problems. Our keen senses attuned us to our surroundings and our metabolism hummed in a healthy place between fuel consumed and energy spent.

Until, about the end of the last century, the game began to change.

With the dawn of digital technology, we seemed to break free of our one-minute-after-the-next existence. We could fax documents in seconds, while delivery before had taken weeks. With word processing, we could cut and paste time.

When the Internet emerged while I worked at ABC News, I no longer had to always schlep downtown to do my job. I could write scripts from home and just press *Send*.

A few years later, a little box came along and we could talk on the phone without a tether. Eventually the box channeled the Internet, connecting us with the world's recorded knowledge and guiding us precisely wherever we wanted to go.

The box and we were soon inseparable.

"A smart phone is the most powerful device in human history," Family Online Safety Institute founder Stephen Balkam remarked as the device began to proliferate, "and you can hold it in the palm of your hand."[1]

But since we didn't evolve with such powerful, synthetic objects, to suddenly be in such close proximity has had unexpected effects.

The longer I work at a screen, the stiffer my back and more my brain feels tied in a knot. I get so engrossed, my dog has to drop her food bowl on my foot to get my attention.

Since we've come to rely so much on Google, GPS, and other digital Alt-Brains, our hard-fought personal assets—from our muscles, to our senses, to our emotions—have been thumped.

Tools initially made to simplify our existence have become more like tyrants, leaving us busier, more frazzled, and less focused than ever before.

Health researchers see trouble ahead now that Alt-Brains do so much of our mental heavy lifting. Says Veronique Bohbot, a neuroscientist in the field of spatial memory, "In the next twenty years I think we're going to see dementia occurring earlier and earlier."[2]

On the other end of the age spectrum, parents of very little kids jump on the digital device bandwagon without knowing the repercussions. "We're conducting the biggest experiment on our children's lives in any of our lifetimes, with virtually no research," worries James Steyer, CEO of the parenting advice group, Common Sense Media.[3]

Don't get me wrong. As a person, a parent, and a science journalist, I see how personal technology has enhanced our lives. I'm as grateful as anyone for our digital devices' amazing abilities. But I'm concerned about what's happening to our own.

Too few of us know that Stanford University devised a whole new science in its Persuasive Technology Lab. "Captology" deliberately pushes our psychological buttons and compels us to compulsively engage with technology. Tristan Harris, who works at Google and trained in the lab, now speaks out about how the practice has set up "a race to the bottom of our brainstems to seduce our instincts."[4]

"What's happening is that we might, in fact, be at a time in our history where we're being domesticated by these great big societal things, such as Facebook and the Internet," says Mark Pagel, a professor of evolutionary biology and member of the Royal Society, which advises the British government on science. "We're being domesticated by them because fewer and fewer of us have to be innovators to get by."[5]

As I write in *The Durable Human Manifesto*, to be "domesticated" is to become like a herd of sheep, devoid of the qualities that make us different from each other.

Author and scientist Aldo Leopold once wrote:

> **Nonconformity is the highest evolutionary attainment of social animals.[6]**

We abandon our individuality at our peril, for if we don't keep up a steady stream of differing new ideas, we offer little to society. At that point, we could actually become *irrelevant* and it may be easier and cheaper to replace us with robots—a process some see as well underway.

Futurist C.G.P. Grey is scaring the bejeezus out of people with his video, "Humans Need Not Apply."[7] He claims we are going the way of horses, which serve no useful function now that we have cars. "As mechanical muscles pushed horses out of the economy, mechanical minds will do the same to humans." We'll soon be shelved—put out to pasture—by artificial intelligence, algorithms and sentient robots which, Grey says, "feel, perceive, or experience subjectively."

Alarmed by the potential of the very technology they had a hand in creating, titans including Microsoft founder Bill Gates, Tesla CEO Elon Musk, and Apple co-founder Steve Wozniak are urging controls on artificial intelligence, especially fearful of military systems that decide for themselves which targets to hunt. Scientist Stephen Hawking warns that "humans, limited by slow biological evolution, couldn't compete and would be superseded by AI."[8]

I believe our species' best chance for survival depends on knowing not only how we compete with machines, but how we *differ* from them.

To screenwriter and philosopher Steven Pressfield, the Self is our deepest being, ever-growing and ever-evolving. As he writes in *The War of Art: Break Through the Blocks and Win Your Inner Creative Battle*, "The Self speaks for the future."

To have a future, it's time we take charge of our Selves.

What It Means to Be Durable

According to Merriam-Webster, the word *durable* is defined as "able to exist for a long time without significant deterioration." Or, as the motto goes, "built to last."

To be a *durable human* is to make full use of your own unique attributes and abilities throughout your lifetime, as you learn from experience, draw strength from nature, and thoughtfully use tools—whether wrenches or data bases.

For too long it's been a one-way street. We've blindly accepted the computerized manna that rained down from the digital heavens. But as renowned biologist Edward O. Wilson cautions, "The more we ignore our common health and welfare, the greater are the many threats to our own species."[9] Or, in the words of C.G.P. Grey: "It's going to be a huge problem if we're not prepared."[10]

This book helps you prepare.

If you read on, you'll be able to fix for yourself what technology has inadvertently dented using solutions as individual as you are.

You'll know how to:

- Find a place to live durably and the time to follow your wild ideas.
- Tune in to the people you care about.
- Maximize your memory.
- Manage your metabolism.
- Eat to compete with tireless gadgets.
- Sleep well in an "I'll sleep when I'm dead" culture.
- Safeguard bio-electrical body parts.
- Help kids to be durable, too.

You'll soon discover that some aspects of your life are quite durable, while others are in need of a tune-up. Pick and choose what you need from the design suggestions on the following pages.

But, you may be thinking, *is it really worth the effort?*

The Chance of You

The Bugatti Veyron is arguably the most elite street-legal sports car in the world. Because it can reach the speed of a jumbo jet at takeoff, a spoiler under the rear window keeps the car *on* the ground. Technicians carry parts for the 1,001-horsepower engine like fine jewelry, in special padded cases. Only a few hundred of the ultra-sleek vehicles have been built since production began in 2005. The most exclusive model costs more than three million U.S. dollars.

Veyrons certainly seem extraordinary until you realize—there is only *one* of you.

Consider that there are about 10^{80} atoms in the known universe.

$$10^{80} = 1,000,000,000,000,000,000,000,000,000,$$
$$000,000,000,000,000,000,000,000,000,$$
$$000,000,000,000,000,000,000,000,000,000$$

That seems like a big number until you consider all the times in human history your ancestors were neither killed nor otherwise prevented from meeting and mating, making the odds you were born:

$$1 \text{ in } 10^{2,685,000}$$

That second number would fill about 22 books the size of this one. It also means the chance you are alive and reading this page is essentially **zero**.[11]

Having beaten *those* odds, shouldn't you care for your Self at least as much as a Veyron owner cares for a car?

Think of the resources you possess at the apex of human evolution. You are composed of interconnected, specialized structures—some liquid, some solid; some as strong as steel, others softer than a pillow.

Inside your brain, 100,000 miles of neural fibers interweave. You can discern millions of colors, half a million sounds, and more than a trillion odors.[12] With a glance you speak volumes, and your hug can heal a broken heart.

Beyond your many senses—the most well-recognized of which are sight, hearing, touch, taste, and smell—you have a treasure trove of other human-only assets, ranging from humor and compassion to delight and intuition.

I once heard a product developer say that "smart" Internet-connected objects "sense everything humans can." Certainly, they do have things like electric eyes, touch sensors, and noise detectors. But does a thermostat have intuition? Can a lightbulb shine with empathy?

Famed oceanographer Sylvia Earle can't do her job without sophisticated autonomous underwater vehicles, but she has no fear machines will take the place of human beings. "Machines are not curious," she says. "They have no sense of humor. They cannot follow hunches. A scientist, or a kid, or anyone, has that capacity to wonder and to explore."[13]

Daniel Goleman coined the term "emotional intelligence" in his 1995 best-seller of the same name. Emotionally intelligent employees use their empathy, enthusiasm and other human-only abilities. Alert, intuitive people are "priceless value creators for employers of any size," says business consultant Liz Ryan.[14]

According to *Forbes* magazine, the most sought-after attributes in an employee are not technical. All are human-centered,[15] including the ability to work in a team, make decisions, and prioritize. Work values have shifted, observes Geoff Colvin in his book, *Humans Are Underrated: What High Achievers Know That Brilliant Machines Never Will*:

> *It used to be that you had to be good at being machine-like.*
> *Now, increasingly, you have to be good at being a person.*[16]

Our human-ness sets us apart from machines. We can't afford to let our hard-fought attributes, intuitions, and instincts be swept away in a tide of digital everything.

Before We Dive In

I have two declarations.

First: although I have written what doctors say on TV, I am not a doctor. This book contains helpful suggestions, not medical advice. What I will report, however, is backed by solid evidence referenced in the back of the book.

Second: this book is only a beginning and not meant to be comprehensive. I hope it will spur your ideas and kick-start a new conversation about what it means to be an effective human being.

But here's exactly why you should keep reading this book:

Faced with the rise of robots and the threat of galloping dementia, if you can do something to shore up your one-of-a-kind Self, *shouldn't you do it?*

CHAPTER 1:
DESIGN YOUR SELF

Make the most of yourself, for that is all there is to you.

Ralph Waldo Emerson, essayist and poet

It wasn't until my middle child went to college that I learned anything about design.

I remember the video from Brian's orientation at Rochester Institute of Technology (RIT). As a camera panned across a room filled with furniture, lamps, knickknacks, and other everyday objects, the narrator observed,

> ### Design is all around us.

Bruce Archer, a mechanical engineer at the British Royal Academy of Arts, penned this definition of design in 1973:

> ***Design is that area of human experience, skill, and knowl-***
> ***edge which is concerned with man's ability to mould [sic]***
> ***his environment to suit his material and spiritual needs.***[28]

In other words, design tends to your body and soul.

A few years before Archer's revelation, RIT introduced Brian's course of study: industrial design. If you have ever flipped on a light switch, sprinkled salt from a shaker, or held a mobile phone, you are familiar with the products of industrial design.

Design to the Rescue

One winter break, Brian came home all excited about collecting used lawn chairs. It was for his class, Guerrilla Design, where students learn how to subtly influence other people's behavior.

His target was a stark walkway on RIT's central campus where students and faculty constantly pass, but rarely stop to socialize. Brian's "Guerrilla Lounge" would attempt to fill that void with what he hoped would be "camaraderie, academic discourse, and relaxation."

A family trip to New York City inspired his idea. While walking along Broadway, we were surprised to see umbrellas and tables set up in the street.

I learned later that, because residents lacked places to rest and socialize, city planners had created "vibrant, social public spaces" out of land that had been used for car lanes.[29] The skinny parks have not impeded car traffic and businesses with store fronts along the repurposed blocks have more customers now than before the transformation.[30]

So, on a spring afternoon, Brian and his classmates clustered thirty-five lawn chairs on a wide expanse of walkway. In less than an hour, students filled the chairs and the air rang with laughter and conversation.

From Brian's experiment we see design is not just about *things*, but about the way things are *done*.

Life, Enhanced

Jared Spool is an expert on usability, which Wikipedia defines as "the ease of use and learnability of a human-made object," such as a book, website or mobile phone. Speaking to a group of mobile phone interface designers, Spool gave this definition:

Design is the rendering of intent.[17]

For our future's sake, we need to look closely at what designers do or don't have in mind.

The most widely acclaimed product of industrial design may be Apple's super-sleek smart phone. Ever since the company introduced Jonathan Ive's creation in 2007, designers have been trying to make all manner of objects smart. Your home may already sport smart lamps, locks, or sprinklers. Soon your walls may listen when you call out for pizza and place the order for you.

Only a few years from now, the world is expected to be packed with a trillion connected objects. This so-called Internet of Things is seen as one of the greatest forces shaping the economic future.[18]

Sensors embedded in everyday objects will "capture data about how we live and what we do," says *Wired* magazine. "We'll be able to choreograph them to respond to our needs, solve our problems, even save our lives."[19]

Already, biohackers are planting smart chips in their skin they hope can be programmed to open doors, start cars, and painlessly monitor blood glucose. "You could imagine a version that could detect the proteins released into the bloodstream during cardiac arrest, and immediately calls an ambulance when it senses you're having a heart attack," writes journalist Dylan Matthews, who implanted a chip in his own hand.[20]

When Mark Rolston was chief creative officer at frog—one of America's most cutting-edge design firms—he called the programmable world, "Life, enhanced."[21] In Rolston's view, as connected appliances, controls, and sensors silently collaborate around us, our minds will be free to dream and innovate.

But is making all objects smart always in the best interest of human beings? Maybe not, says Allen Chochinov, founding partner of the go-to industrial designers' website, Core 77.

During a lecture at RIT, Chochinov urged design students not to eliminate human input. He lamented: "Today, if you want to know what's wrong with a car engine, you can't even open it. You need to plug in a computer. High schools are dropping shop class. Soon, no one will know how to do anything."[22]

Pondering Chochinov's comments and Rolston's notion of "Life, enhanced," I asked Brian, "How are we 'enhanced' if good stuff like our muscles and reasoning aren't used and we don't have any skills? Shouldn't design 'enhance' human beings?"

"Well," he mused, "we're taught that what we design should always enhance people somehow. A better word may be 'promote.' Design should *promote* humanity and the great things only humans can do."

Thus was born my concept of *durable human design*—the making and doing of things that promote and advance one's ability to be an effective, contributing human in a complex and increasingly digital world.

In *The Manifesto*, I write that you need three keys to unlock your ability to be a durable human. They are the three jewels in the *Triple Crown of Durability*.

The Triple Crown of Durability

 Jewel 1 is **SELF-RELIANCE**. Durable humans have skills so they can do things for themselves.

 Jewel 2 stands for **GENUINE RELATIONSHIPS**. Durable humans connect with other people for mutual benefit.

 Jewel 3 depicts **CURIOSITY**. Durable humans recognize, liberate, and pursue their own wild ideas.

Durable human designs promote at least one jewel of the Triple Crown.

Robert Zarr, for example, is a pediatrician in Washington, D.C., who saw in his practice that too many kids were struggling to be healthy and rarely got a chance to go out and play. That's why he decided to write prescriptions for going to the park. He also inventoried the amenities of every playground, park, and field in the city to help people choose according to their interests.

By giving D.C. citizens the skills and knowledge to maintain their own mental and physical health, Dr. Zarr's designs promote Jewel 1 of the Triple Crown.

Brian's pop-up lounge advanced Jewel 2 by giving people a place to build relationships as they laughed, told stories, and relaxed.

Peace activist and Vietnamese Buddhist monk Thích Nhất Hạnh went to Google with a Jewel 2 idea he calls compassion-check. Like spell-check, compassion-check would alert you if you typed a potentially hurtful word.

Before his visit, he told *The Guardian,*

> *When I talk to Google and the other [Silicon Valley] companies, I will tell them to use their intelligence and goodwill to help us create the kind of instruments to come back to ourselves, heal ourselves... We do not have to reject or throw away all these devices but can make good use of them.*[23]

Student designer Aaron Horowitz was curious if he could help kids with juvenile diabetes, so he dreamed up Jerry the Bear[24]—a product of Jewel 3.

The cute and cuddly stuffed animal has sensors that allow the kids to painlessly learn how to give themselves injections. On a screen on Jerry's tummy, the kids can also play games about managing their condition.

Durable human designs energize people.

At Chicago's O'Hare airport, the ceiling and walls of a long hallway have been blanketed with pulsating, multi-colored lights. Now, rather than being stultified, travelers look forward to discovering the next delightful hue.

Detroit's airport goes a step further. Along its mid-terminal hallway, glass-paneled walls flash colors that change along with dramatic music.

In Portland, Oregon, Morgan Gray won the Triple Crown of Durability when she revolutionized the laundry business. Her Spin Laundry Lounge does for dirty clothes what car-sharing does for driving. Morgan turned an old metal shop into an attractive space where people can do together what has been an isolating, monotonous chore. By providing the world's most energy- and water-conserving washers and dryers, she also cares for the planet. In her Spin Café, customers also enjoy camaraderie, good food, and midnight happy hours.

Why Be Curious?

The first two jewels in the Triple Crown may be obvious. Whether it's when the power goes out or a natural disaster swamps the system, you know that times will come when you must rely on yourself.

Likewise, we are hardwired to realize our species can't survive unless we cooperate to solve mutual problems, as has always been the case. "If we didn't do those things on the savanna 100,000 years ago, we died," observes *Humans Are Underrated* author Geoff Colvin.[25]

But *curiosity?*

I once asked Brian if he thinks creativity is at the center of all original endeavors. His answer surprised me: "If you don't care to pursue an idea, it can't come to fruition. That's why, even before you're creative, you need to be *curious.*"

Not long after our conversation, I was in the audience at a celebration of *Cosmos,* National Geographic's update of the 1980 Carl Sagan TV series about the universe. The new host is Neil deGrasse Tyson, a personable astrophysicist who is also the director of New York's Hayden Planetarium.

At the event, Tyson was asked how he views the future prospects for humanity. This was his answer:

> *That depends on how any one person would answer this question: "Have you been curious lately?"*

Curiosity pushes us to where no one has thought before. Our lifeline to the future, curiosity keeps humans in the game. With curiosity, we are doers and makers, not simply users.

In corporate settings, curiosity "breathes new life into organizations," says John Bell, global managing director of Social@Ogilvy public relations firm. "Most companies need a curious workforce to source enough new thinking. Sometimes innovation can be the job of the few," Bell continues. "But more often, these days, our best bet is to make curiosity an ideal for the entire workforce."[26]

Durable Role Models

In the feature film *The Martian,* actor Matt Damon plays NASA astronaut Mark Watney. His crew members accidentally leave him on Mars to fend for himself. In so doing, he does glean help from leftover laptops, but his talent with duct tape is equally crucial. His human-only sense of humor props up his spirits and his ingenuity transforms barren Martian dust into fertile, food-bearing soil.

The Watney character springs from the imagination of real-life computer programmer Andy Weir, whose dad is an accelerator physicist and mom is an electrical engineer. But Weir is such a skilled writer, he enables the average viewer to understand dense technical topics that range from orbital mechanics to oxygen synthesis. The world discovered the Watney story after the generous Weir posted it for free on his website.

If durable humans, as I write in *The Manifesto,* "fully engage their brains and, when they need to, the tools at hand"—don't we all strive to be Weirs and Watneys?

Many durable human designs will incorporate the tools of technology, which should always serve—and never impede or supersede—the human user.

We need to be watchful for products we're told are helpful, but actually aren't in our best interest. An automatic buckle that expands your belt when you eat too much does not promote human durability.

Likewise, we don't need a drone that can walk the dog to deprive us of one of our best opportunities to move.

Just because there's an unbreakable case so babies can play with smartphones in their cribs doesn't mean it's a good idea to buy it. Nor does it help a toddler in the long run to be trained on a potty with a built-in tablet.

But since there's little chance these kinds of products will stop being made, it's up to you to know what supports durability and what doesn't.

With that in mind, you don't need to wait for professionals to design your durable lifestyle. You can do it yourself.

The Laws of Self-Design

When you choose what to wear in the morning, you design your look for the day. The foods you pop in your grocery cart design your meals for the week. The location where you choose to live designs your lifestyle.

Thus, we arrive at The First Law of Self-Design:

Everyone is a designer

Now hold on there, you might say. *I can't design because I'm not creative.*

My cousin tried that reasoning with me, too.

I remember the day I visited her office after a major renovation. The colors and textures all harmonized, evoking a sense of peace and order. From light fixtures to furniture to carpets to drapes, the attention to detail was obvious. Even the elevator walls were covered in gorgeous bird's eye maple.

My cousin had overseen every aspect.

"What about how you juggled all those swatches and contractors?" I asked her. "Look at the final product. You're *definitely* creative."

Which leads us to The Second Law of Self-Design:

Everyone is creative

Creativity is the lighting on your personal path to durability. "When you follow your own true north, you create new opportunities, meet different people, have different experiences, and create a different life," writes Ted Robinson in *Out of Our Minds: Learning to be Creative*.[27]

Once you understand that both laws apply to you, designing a durable lifestyle can be easy, but only if you know what your highly evolved body can do for you and what you may inadvertently do to your body.

CHAPTER 2:

ACTIVATE

I only went out for a walk and finally concluded to stay out until sundown, for going out, I found, was really going in.

John Muir, nature conservationist

It was a typical London morning and twenty-year-old Chris Staniforth was about to apply for a job. But as he stepped into the employment center, he dropped dead.

"He had probably been on all night—on the computer at his desk, on Facebook, or gaming," the young man's shaken father told the BBC. "He lived for his Xbox. I never dreamed he was in any danger."[31]

Although Chris had no apparent health problems, he had developed a deep vein thrombosis, or DVT. A DVT is a clot that forms in the deep veins of the lower leg, thigh, pelvis, or even the arm. If a piece of the clot breaks off, it can flow through the bloodstream toward vital organs such as the heart.

In Chris's case, the clot blocked blood flow to his lung, technically known as a pulmonary embolism. The chance of dying from a pulmonary embolism is one in three.

Anyone who sits for more than a few hours—whether on a plane, at a desk, or in front of a console—risks a DVT. The best way to avoid one is to regularly get up and move.

"Try to stop every hour or so and just walk around for a few minutes to keep the blood circulating," says Dr. Phil Ragno, director of cardiovascular health and wellness at Winthrop University Hospital in Mineola, New York.

Even if you're stuck on a long plane flight or in an all-day meeting, moving your feet will boost your circulation and help prevent clots. An easy way is to lift your feet a few inches off the floor and trace the letters of the alphabet with the tips of your toes.[32]

Because Chris Staniforth's dad still has a warm place in his heart for the video games his son loved so much, he advised parents on ABC News: "Don't stop your child from playing the games. Just be aware. [Tell them], 'Enjoy it, but take a break.'"

The Sedentary Dilemma

For most of human existence, we were almost constantly active, whether to fetch food, prepare it, or simply shiver for warmth. But when the digital age dawned, most of civilization sat down. People began spending hours—even days—hardly moving a muscle.

When you don't use your muscles, they shut down. "The muscles go as silent as those of a dead horse," says biomedical researcher Marc Hamilton of Louisiana State University.[33]

Besides upping your risk of several types of cancer, if you are too sedentary you set the stage for insidious metabolic diseases. *Metabolism* is the scientific word for the chemical interplay of your body processes.

When you stop moving, your metabolism slows down, you burn fewer calories and produce fewer of the enzymes you need for, in Hamilton's words, "vacuuming up fat out of the bloodstream."

A metabolic disease that's become a scourge is type 2 diabetes, which now afflicts nine percent of all adults worldwide.[34] Once called "adult onset diabetes," the name changed when so many children developed the condition.[35]

"Excessive sitting is a lethal activity,"[36] concludes James Levine, a Mayo Clinic physician specializing in the emerging field of sedentary physiology. "The human body was not designed to be idle. The public usually associates these [metabolic] health problems with eating too much, not with sitting too much. My experience with people who struggle with their weight has led me to think that sitting habits might be just as pernicious."[37]

Take the new twist on an American favorite pastime: binge-watching TV—a term that only entered the dictionary in 2014.[38] Studies from earlier don't bode well. One shows that men who regularly sat for six or more hours in their leisure time had a death rate 20 percent higher than men who sat down for three hours or less. The death rate was twice as high for similarly inactive women.[39]

But the sedentary predicament reaches far beyond our leisure time. All around the world, those who had active jobs such as farming now work in desk-bound, sit-down settings, such as banks and call centers.[40]

With millions of people inadvertently thwarting the metabolism of their own highly evolved bodies, it is costing us all.

Almost 20 percent of America's gross national product, for instance, is spent on healthcare, much of it to treat the one of every two adults who has a preventable chronic disease.[41] According to economic projections, the sedentary status quo threatens to run the country right into the ground.

"The U.S. economy will collapse if we keep spending the money we're spending on medical services," says Richard J. Jackson, a physician, University of California at Los Angeles (UCLA) professor, former federal health official, and author of the book *Designing Healthy Communities.*[42]

Your Loyal Body

If you think your get-up-and-go has been gone for too long, your body is ready to help you bounce back.

Overweight women who become slightly more active begin to produce more of the hormones and proteins that protect against breast cancer. Evidence from many other studies shows that being more physically active helps ward off cancers elsewhere in the body, including the colon, lung, uterus, and prostate.[43]

Since exercise helps your body process sugars in your bloodstream, being more active can help to avoid—or at least better control—type 2 diabetes and the life-threatening damage the disease can cause your nerves, skin, heart, and kidneys.[44]

You catch fewer colds when you move more. "The most powerful weapon someone has during cold season is to go out, on a near-daily basis, and put in at least a thirty-minute brisk walk," says David Nieman of the Human Performance Laboratory at Appalachian State University.[45]

Getting regular exercise is nothing to sneeze at when you consider it may cut by one-third your chance of succumbing to what the U.S. Department of Health and Human Services calls "early death."[46]

Workplace research also shows that employees who exercise before or during work are better at meeting deadlines and get along better with coworkers.[47]

"Employers who are ahead of the game in offering proper on-site [exercise] facilities actually get less from their employees on days that they *don't* exercise," says Jo Coulson of the University of Bristol.[48]

The financial advice firm Motley Fool employs a full-time Fitness Fool who encourages workers to stretch, twist, and move throughout the day. The company also offers exercise classes, yoga, and meditation. No junky snacks or sugary sodas are sold in vending machines, but cats and dogs are brought in to dispense cuddles during high stress periods.

"Nurses tell us we are the healthiest employees they have seen," reports Motley Fool Director of Office Culture Melissa Malinowski. "You're going to be more alert and work more efficiently if you're healthy."[49]

At shoe company New Balance, staff members who participated in a study where they had short bursts of physical activity every thirty minutes felt they could concentrate better and were more engaged with their work.[50]

But what exactly is this "exercise" we're all supposed to be getting?

Exercise FAQs

In the digital age, exercise and exercise equipment attempt to simulate what humans used to do naturally in the course of a day.

Stripping the skin off animals they caught for dinner used to be how people built strong muscles. Today, activities where you pull or push against a force are called muscle-strengthening exercise and include yoga and lifting weights. Weeding, pushing a lawn mower, and other types of yard work also strengthen muscles.

In the old, old days, human hearts got pumping with things like out-running a saber-toothed cat.

Now, hearts and lungs get a workout through aerobic exercise, such as jumping jacks and salsa dancing. Jogging and riding bicycles are aerobic, too.

The U.S. Centers for Disease Control and Prevention (CDC) tell us an adult needs at least a half hour of moderate-intensity aerobic activity, five days a week. That's a total of 150 minutes, or about how long it takes to watch a feature film.

Moderate-intensity aerobics include walking at the speed of at least three miles per hour, ballroom dancing, and doubles tennis.

If you put in more effort, you can spend less time. By doing vigorous-intensity aerobic activities, such as running at least six miles per hour or playing singles tennis, you can slim down your weekly minimum to seventy-five total minutes.

We are told to exercise major muscle groups—including legs, hips, back, abdomen, chest, shoulders, and arms—at least twice a week.

At my dad's senior living community, I joined him for a class that fulfilled that requirement. For nearly an hour, we stretched rubber exercise bands, lifted hand weights, and almost constantly moved our feet. The next day, I knew exactly which muscles I hadn't worked in a while.

By the way, my father is ninety-two years old, but because of all the exercise, good nutrition, and camaraderie where he lives, he's more durable now than when he moved there.

Kids need twice as much physical activity as adults do: a full hour per day, at least five days of the week. Good old running around, playing, and climbing qualify as both aerobic *and* muscle-strengthening, plus offer many other benefits we will talk about later.

Older people need to get back on the kids' schedule of five hours of physical activity a week. That extra half hour a day shouldn't be seen as a burden, but as an investment. The durability payoff for older people is that exercise improves balance, stamina, flexibility, joint mobility, agility, walking, and physical coordination, says U.S. Surgeon General Vivek Murthy.[51]

Investing your time in exercise is also a hedge against senility. In a study of fifty- to eighty-year-old Americans, those who walked forty-five minutes, three days a week, over a year's time increased brain volume by two percent, while the brains of non-walkers *shrank* by one-and-a-half percent.[52]

Isn't it gratifying to realize that whenever you take a stride, you're pumping up your brain just a little bit?

To make exercise easier to swallow, your daily dose can be subdivided into bouts as brief as ten minutes.[53]

"Going to the gym is not the only thing you can do. Things like taking the stairs and walking to the bus stop do add up," reports Nicole Glazer, an epidemiology genetics researcher at Boston University School of Medicine. "It's important to exercise even if you do not have time to do so, and you can fit it into your day."[54]

Physical activity recommendations for all age groups are at Health.gov/paguidelines.

Don't be Full of Sit

When Day Martin was a data analyst, she hurt her back in a car accident. Gradually, she got better, until the only time she still had pain was sitting down at work. To take the pressure off her back, she recalls, "The Internet recommended I try a standing desk."[55]

But the desks for sale weren't right for her workspace, which was— as it is for untold millions of others—a cubicle. That's when Martin decided to design, and eventually sell, her *own* desk.

Not only does her version help relieve back pain and fit in a cubicle, it saves people valuable time. Martin includes a penny that busy customers can use as a screwdriver to assemble her StandSteady desk in only two minutes.

So, simply by putting together Martin's desk, you can achieve Jewel 1: having skills to do things for yourself.

The way I used to start my day was to take the dog for a half-hour walk. After that, I'd have breakfast then sit at my computer. Later, I'd sit behind the steering wheel and drive to a meeting, sit through the meeting, then come home and sit down for dinner. In the evening, I'd likely sit down to chat, read, or watch something on TV.

That was a *lot* of sitting.

"The robotic lifestyle of just incorporating thirty minutes of physical activity into your day, and spending the other twenty-three-and-a-half hours idle, does not produce the healthy profile we're looking for," says Mark Tremblay, director of Healthy Active Living and Obesity Research at Children's Hospital of Eastern Ontario in Canada.

Through his work, Dr. Tremblay has determined there are two types of people. The *Prolonger* is a person who sits for prolonged periods of time. The *Breaker* tends to take breaks, as he says, "if only to move about briefly during seated activities."[56] Because the breaker regularly gets up to putter, he or she moves more over a day's time than the Prolonger who tends to remain sitting down.

So, if you're a Breaker and find reasons to get up from your chair throughout the day, you'll be more durable in the long run because— like a tortoise, not a hare—you'll slowly but surely be more active.

Durable Human Designs for Moving More

It doesn't take much to add flashes of activity to your day.

At the office

- Use the stairs instead of an elevator or escalator. Start by walking up just one flight.
- Stand when you talk on the phone.
- Instead of texting or emailing a co-worker, walk over and speak directly. If the conversation will be extensive, suggest walking and talking.
- Walk during your lunch break.
- Use a standing desk. I like Day Martin's portable StandSteady because it's so lightweight I can carry it with me wherever I work.

At home

- Stand up and walk when you talk on the phone. Cook more and buy less take-out food.
- Instead of using a TV remote, get up and change the channel by hand.
- Stand while you watch TV. Strengthen muscle groups by lifting hand weights, doing squats against a wall, or using a treadmill or rebounder.
- Step to the beat of the U.S. Surgeon General's walking playlist at Pandora.com.

When you drive

- To take more steps, park in a space at the far end of the lot or a few blocks from your destination.
- To increase arm strength:
  - Carry your groceries from the store to your car.
  - Pull the trunk closed rather than hitting the automatic-close button.

You might also try getting from here to there without driving.

CHAPTER 3

CHOOSE YOUR PLACE

The opposite of freedom is when we don't have any choices.

Peter Norton, author of *Fighting Traffic*

Before the automobile was king, neighborhoods were different.

"Nothing was designed to be particularly beneficial to cars. It was a greener, quieter, less intrusive world," writer and humorist Bill Bryson recalls in his memoir, *The Life and Times of the Thunderbolt Kid.*

When Bryson was growing up in the 1950s, sidewalks lined typical American streets, which were arranged in a grid. Every other kid walked or rode a bicycle to school. Only four in every hundred children were overweight, as opposed to seventeen in every hundred today.[57]

But after World War II, walkable communities gave way to a new kind of design: *suburbs,* which were predicated on the sedentary practice of driving.

In a typical suburb, single-family homes line both sides of a long, curving street that often ends in a dead-end cul-de-sac. Gone is the street grid, along with the ability to walk between neighborhoods.

"A simple one-mile trip to a close-by friend now becomes a roundabout journey that involves traveling along a suburban roadway and back into another neighborhood, possibly tripling the driving distance," explains civil engineer and active living advocate Fionnuala Quinn.

I first met Fionnuala *(pronounced Finn-OO-lah)* in a workshop where ordinary citizens learned about the local transportation system. Participants were asked to recall their first trips on public transit. Recollections continued around the room until someone said, in a delightful Irish brogue, "I started riding the public bus home alone from school when I was four."

That was Fionnuala, now my friend and bicycling companion. Fionnuala follows in the footsteps of her Irish mother and grandmother, who received better educations because they got to better schools by bicycle.

Today, Fionnuala is a civil engineer in the United States, where she continues to travel by foot, bike, and bus. But since she lives in the suburbs, she is an outlier. As she observes, "This most ordinary and sensible means of local transportation can be an oddity in a travel culture that has developed around minivans and SUVs."

Fionnuala understands how having no way to travel other than by car works against durability: "Children, younger teens, and older people are frequently stranded if their only option is being driven and there's no way to get themselves around."[58]

America's so-called love affair with the car did not spring from the desires of ordinary Americans. In fact, when cars were first introduced early in the 1900s, the public viewed motorized vehicles as a menace, especially to children, who at that time played happily in the streets.

According to technology historian Peter Norton, within a decade of coming to understand the public's negative view of cars, automobile-related industries devised an advertising campaign aimed at changing public perception. They painted a utopian picture of people who could drive anywhere they wanted in cars of their own.

The campaign paid off. As Norton points out in his book *Fighting Traffic: The Dawn of the Motorized Age in the American City*,[59] by the end of the twentieth century, almost 91 percent of Americans had eschewed other forms of travel and were driving to work as single occupants in their own vehicles.

But Motordom didn't turn out as perfect as advertised. Yes, cars have led to a tremendous increase in personal mobility and economic growth, but excessive use has also damaged the land, the air, and human health.

"The inactivity-producing convenience, often violent speed, and toxic exhaust of our cars have contributed mightily to the circumstance that, for the first time in history, the current generation of youth will live shorter lives than their parents," declares urban planner and architect Jeff Speck in his book, *Walkable City: How Downtown Can Save America, One Step at a Time.*

Speck directly places the blame: "The car and its minions have unnecessarily distorted the way that design decisions are made in American communities."

With all that in mind, Peter Norton urges us to "realign the story of the past to go toward the future you want." In other words: throw off the driving status quo.

Well, that doesn't apply to me, you may be thinking. *I have to drive to get where I'm going. Besides, I like my car.*

Yes, of course, most people including myself drive either a little or a lot because of their circumstances. But it's important to remember—when it's possible—getting around in other ways could help you to be more durable.

Thanks to the human-only sense of ingenuity, the pendulum is swinging back. Land planners, developers, and businesses are following Dr.

Richard Jackson's prescription for reversing the sedentary epidemic and "building physical activity irresistibly into people's lives."[60] For instance, buildings with features such as wide, well-lit stairways entice people to use them.

What Is "Walkable"?

Most people will stay with an organized fitness class for about six months, at which point they lapse into their former state of inactivity. So says Mark Fenton, Olympic race walker turned active living advocate. According to Fenton, the only way a fitness routine can "stick" among your daily habits is if you "make exercise a no-brainer"— something you don't even have to think about.[61]

Enter: humanity's earliest form of transportation.

What's great about walking is that, unless you're on a treadmill, you can actually *get somewhere*.

As such, by simply catching a bus or strolling to the store you are considered "active." Though it might not feel like exercise per se, walking back and forth can easily give you the half hour of moderate aerobic activity you need for the day. That's also why people who use public transportation generally weigh less than drivers.[62]

Whether in the city or the suburbs, people who walk where they live also have lower rates of diabetes.[63] "When you live in a neighborhood designed to encourage people to be more active, you are in fact more likely to be more active," says Marisa Creatore, a Canadian epidemiologist with Toronto's Centre for Research on Inner City Health.

Sidewalks are still quite popular in America. According to the National Association of Realtors, eighty-five percent of new U.S. home buyers say they look specifically for the ability to walk and use public transportation.[64]

Why walking works so well is because it comes naturally. Jeff Speck's book quotes Enrique Peñalosa, former mayor of Bogota, Columbia:

> *God made us walking animals – pedestrians. As a fish needs to swim, a bird to fly, a deer to run, we need to walk, not in order to survive, but to be happy.*[65]

Physical activity is baked into neighborhoods that are walkable, which—according to architect and planner Rick Phillips—share these basic characteristics:[66]

- Automobiles may be present, but are traveling at lower speeds.
- Walkers and cyclists have a greater sense of safety and comfort because they feel less threatened by motorized vehicles.
- Public transportation is usually nearby, as are schools, shopping, and parks.

Your family has a greater chance at a durable lifestyle if you live in a neighborhood where sidewalks connect to a good school than if you live near the same school but walking isn't possible.

A handy tool that can help your personal land use planning is Walkscore.com. The website can give you a rough idea of the walkability of neighborhoods in countries including the U.S., Canada, Australia, and New Zealand. Plug in an address and you can learn whether there are nearby features such as schools, parks, coffee shops, and grocery stores. You'll also learn how long it takes to reach them by car, foot, bus, or bicycle.

A Note about Bicycles

A few years ago, I rediscovered the joys of cycling. Now, I use a nearby bike trail to ride to meetings. I love to see the crimson cardinals darting through the underbrush and hear the music of rushing creeks.

It turns out that sense of elation is a scientifically proven phenomenon. Generally, people who bicycle to destinations are happier with the trip than those who travel by car. "Exercise elevates your mood," reports Eric Morris, a Clemson University active transportation researcher.

But, there's even more to the durable story. As Morris points out: "You get that sense of mastery and proving to yourself that you're skilled, rather than just sitting and riding in a bus or a car."[67]

When you cycle, you achieve the first jewel of the Triple Crown because you are Self-propelled.

Living in a community where you can walk and bike also can increase your financial durability.[68] "Transportation is the second largest expense for families, but few consider these costs when choosing a place to live," according to the Center for Neighborhood Technology. Families who have the option to walk, bicycle, or take public transit can save money because they may need fewer (or no) cars and have to buy gasoline less often (or never).

These tools can help you choose a durable place to live:

- The Housing & Transportation Affordability Index gauges affordability based on housing and transportation costs. See DurableHuman.com/H+TIndex.
- You can also include the cost of food, taxes, healthcare, child-care, and other necessities by using the Economic Policy Institute's Family Budget Calculator. See DurableHuman.com/FamilyBudgetCalculator.

The color of a durable lifestyle is almost always green. Dozens of studies show that people feel more optimistic when they can be around trees and other vegetation.

Removed from sirens, horns, and screeching brakes, we are measurably less anxious. Those who live where they can walk also tend to be more trusting of their neighbors, more involved with community projects, and less likely to watch a lot of TV.[69]

In Portland, Oregon, some neighborhoods have "adopted" their local intersections. Neighbors come up with a design they paint onto the pavement, then add shared amenities around it, such as playhouses, solar-powered tea stations, and mini lending libraries.[70]

"These are all about bringing people together, giving people the empowerment and freedom to express themselves where they live, and creating a special place that reflects who lives here," says Greg Raisman, a traffic safety specialist in Portland's Active Transportation Department.[71]

In parts of Portland plagued by violence, when young people are involved in intersection adoptions, there is measurably more social cohesion and a greater sense of community ownership.[72]

Kids and Curiosity

In a study of school-aged girls living in Chicago public housing, those in apartments with views of nature can concentrate better and have greater self-control than girls without views of vegetation.[73]

Other studies show that a daily dose of nature can reduce a child's reliance on medicine to treat attention-deficit/hyperactivity disorder (ADHD).[74]

Being able to walk and play may be a child's best chance to defeat the CDC's dire prediction that one in every three of them will be diabetic in adulthood.[75] Yet, many parents are reluctant to let their kids roam—even if those same parents spent hours playing outside when they were children.

Like flowers without water, kids wilt when they don't have enough time outdoors. They can even develop mental and physical symptoms, as author Richard Louv points out in his seminal book, *Last Child in the Woods: Saving Our Children from Nature-Deficit Disorder.*

Louv has his own thoughts about ADHD medication: "Could it be that some of the increases we see in prescriptions has to do with the fact that we took away the calming effect of nature in the first place?"

Not allowing kids time outdoors deprives them of "lessons they can't learn in the classroom," UCLA's Dr. Richard Jackson told me.

Outside in the sun and wind, the information kids have consumed inside has a chance to percolate. They have wild, unscheduled time for the third jewel of the Triple Crown: following their curiosity.

Through play, kids become familiar with their own bodies' strengths and abilities. Besides physical coordination, they boost their powers of concentration. They learn quickly what happens if they don't pay attention when climbing a tree.

According to Louv, kids who play with other kids in a free-form, natural space (as opposed to planned playgrounds) are more accepting of people who look different from themselves or are a different gender.[76]

When kids are free to play without adult direction, they tend to invent their own games, which in Louv's words, "has something to do with developing entrepreneurs in the future."

Canadian artist and outdoor educator Marghanita Hughes designs books and activities that help young imaginations soar. Her *Storytelling with Nature* e-book, for instance, shows how kids can make lovable little characters out of sticks, acorn tops, and other bits they find outside.

The part of the brain we use for navigation is called the hippocampus. When kids think through where they need to go, their hippocampi get a workout right along with them.

Kids who are physically active also tend to listen better in the class-room, which may be the main reason why school systems around the world are encouraging kids to walk and bike to school.

In the United States, the government-funded Safe Routes to School (SRTS) program sponsors International Walk to School Day in October and National Bike to School Day in May.

SRTS also pays for or otherwise supports creating safer ways for kids to walk and bike. Sometimes, a few cans of paint or yards of concrete are all it takes to connect a neighborhood to a school.

Efforts by SRTS and other groups such as the Foundation for Environmental Education's Eco-Schools are beginning to pay off. Between 2007 and 2012, the number of American elementary-age kids who walked to school increased by 27 percent.[77]

Pediatrician Jason Mendoza and his research team at Seattle Children's Hospital are measuring the activity levels and weight of kids who walk and bike. As he says,

We're hoping these healthy habits get engrained and become a part of lifestyles moving forward.[78]

Pre-teens who can safely cycle to school love the added independence and few extra winks of sleep they may get when they don't have to catch the school bus.

Because today's high school students are able to spend time together online, they aren't as eager to drive as teens were before the Internet. Walking and biking help teens stay in shape. They also have more down time with friends and can avoid the hassle and expense of driving.

Older kids can also benefit from learning to use public transportation. Because the county where I live—Fairfax, in Virginia—understands that, it became one of the first in the U.S. where middle school and high school kids can ride the county bus system for free.

Durable Human Designs to Increase Kids' Self-Reliance

Because kids under age ten usually don't have the judgment to cross a street safely, they need older guides.[79] Children who can't walk or bike to school with a parent, older sibling, or guardian may be able to join a "walking school bus"—a neighborhood walking group organized by parents or schools.

In suburban northern Virginia, Jeff Anderson is a stay-at-home dad who became a Pied Piper on wheels. Because there was no place for his kids to lock up their bikes at school, he asked the principal for a rack. When she installed it, the Anderson kids wanted their friends to ride, too. That's when Anderson started leading his own and the neighborhood kids to school on a "bike train."

Because they build skills as well as relationships, kids achieve at least two jewels of the Triple Crown when they take part in bike trains and walking school buses. To learn more about both, go to Durablehuman.com/BikeWalk.

If you want your young loved one to independently walk or bike, make sure to:

- Brush up on the safety basics. Read the parent information on WalkBiketoSchool.org.
- Watch these kid-friendly videos with your child:
    - If walking: DurableHuman.com/KidsWalkSafeVideo
    - If cycling: DurableHuman.com/KidsBikeSafeVideo
- Map out a safe route on paper or with tools such as Google Maps.

- Size your child's helmet and bike, then check to be sure:
  - Tires are full
  - Brakes operate
  - Chains are tight
  - Seat is adjusted and tight
  - Horn or bell is audible
  - Reflectors are on the front, back, and wheels

It may be easier and safer for kids to carry items to school in the bike's front basket or rear rack, instead of a backpack.

Because Jeff Anderson didn't want a heavy backpack to be a barrier to a child's riding to school, on his bike trains, he piles backpacks in a trailer attached to his bike—the same trailer he used to take his kids for rides when they were toddlers.

If you live in a place where kids don't usually walk or bike, you can change the status quo. Safe Routes to School can help you start an encouragement campaign. Get the information at DurableHuman. com/TakeInitiative.

Try to team up with like-minded energetic people as I did with Jeff and Fionnuala.

And always remember the sage words of anthropologist, Margaret Mead:

> *Never doubt that a small group of committed people can change the world. Indeed, it is the only thing that ever has.*

And now, a word from your skeleton.

CHAPTER 4:

RESPECT YOUR STRUCTURE

If you truly get in touch with a piece of carrot, you get in touch with the soil, the rain, the sunshine.

Thích Nhất Hanh, Buddhist monk and peace activist

As the sheriff waded into the chaotic scene, stretchers of sobbing, bloody people streamed past. They had come from as far away as India to this Texas suburb. Most were wearing traditional silken garb–followers of Jainism, an ancient Indian religion that strives for a state of non-violence for all living beings.

Moments before, the visitors had been praying in a room above the garage of a two-story home–there to dedicate a glittering, new altar.

That's when the floor gave way.

"A mechanical overload of the structure," the fire marshal later declared. Forty people had been jammed into a space designed to hold only seven.

The same thing can happen when you overload your body. If you exceed your skeleton's natural carrying capacity, your bones, joints, and body functions could soon break down.

The durable reality is that your bones are made to support a certain weight range for your particular height. Going beyond that range is when the trouble starts.

Chances are you'll notice problems first in your weight-bearing joints—most likely, your ankles or knees. Because your heart must work harder to push blood through extra fatty tissue, your blood pressure will probably rise and you'll tire more easily.

Because the steady hum of your metabolism is thrown off balance, whole-body ailments may be triggered, such as heart disease or type 2 diabetes.

To avoid this, respect your structure.

How Calories Count

In the old, old days, between coping with the elements and scrounging for food, we humans burned lots and lots of calories.

As recently as a hundred years ago, most jobs involved physical labor, so a typical 155-pound man would most likely have expended at least 200 calories in a half hour. Today, the same-sized person working on a computer burns barely 50 calories.[80]

That is why each calorie *matters*.

Just as a Veyron owner wouldn't pour dirty crude down the car's velvety gullet, you need to pay attention to how you fuel your unique Self.

"We don't need large amounts of sugar, fat, and salt, particularly if we're going to be sitting at a keyboard all day long,"[81] says UCLA's Dr. Richard Jackson.

But even here in the digital age, the best foods to eat are what have always enabled our species to survive and thrive: those that come from the earth and oceans, where nature conveniently packages the nutrients we need for durability.

In fact, fruits and vegetables are considered "powerhouse" foods, because they are the best at protecting you from chronic disease.[82]

A single garlic clove, for instance, bursts with vitamins B6 and C, plus the minerals phosphorus, zinc, and selenium.

The positive punch of spinach comes not only from muscle- and blood-strengthening iron, but also co-enzymes, cancer-fighting antioxidants, and the rare vitamin K, needed for blood clotting and heart protection.

Beans—the low-fat, affordable staple of meals the world over—provide protein, fiber, B vitamins, and the minerals iron, folate, and magnesium.

Foods are most nutritionally potent when they change as little as possible from field to fork. The more processed, the less the nutritional value, according to CDC dietary guidelines.[83]

In 2016, the CDC recommended a healthy eating pattern that includes:

- Vegetables, in as much variety as possible, including beans, peas, and potatoes. The CDC specifically mentioned veggies that are dark green, red, and orange.
- Fruits, as-picked if possible, such as a whole apple rather than applesauce with added sugar.
- Grains, at least half of which should be whole and unprocessed, such as brown rice (as opposed to white rice, which has been bleached and processed).
- Non-fat and low-fat dairy products, including milk, yogurt, and cheese.
- Protein foods, again in a wide variety, including lean meats and poultry, eggs, nuts, seeds, foods made from soy, as well as protein-packed beans and peas.

- Oils, because they supply essential fatty acids and vitamin E. Food prepared with liquid oils such as olive, canola, and corn is preferable to that made with solids, including butter, stick margarine, shortening, lard, and coconut oil.

The CDC gives a nod to Dr. Jackson by recommending we limit what we eat each day to:

- Less than 10 percent of total calories from added sugars.
- Less than 10 percent of total calories from saturated fats.
- No more sodium than the equivalent of one teaspoon of salt.

We are told to shy away from foods that combine too much of that unhealthy triumvirate of saturated fat, salt and sugar. Those include American favorites such as hamburgers, pizza, tacos, and ice cream—which are almost always made with full-fat meat and dairy products.

What you drink also matters. Since 60 percent of your body is made up of water, that is your drink of choice for durability. By including water in its guidelines, the CDC hopes to nudge Americans away from their habit of consuming 20 percent of daily calories in the form of soda and other sugary drinks.

The *ChooseMyPlate* graphic is based on the U.S. dietary guidelines and depicts the foods we should eat in what proportions.

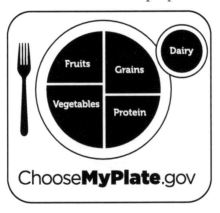

Notice that half the plate is covered by fruits and vegetables—all supplied, ready to eat, by nature.

Interestingly, some advice in the guidelines speaks directly to durability.

The CDC promotes Jewel 1 by recommending that Americans learn the skills of "gardening, cooking, meal planning, and label reading."

The agency acknowledges the effects of the digital age by encouraging individuals to "limit screen time and time spent being sedentary."

BMI Basics

To know how many pounds your own frame of bones is built to carry, you need to calculate your Body Mass Index (BMI). The BMI is a measure of the weight range where your body functions best and is considered "normal" for your particular height. You can determine your BMI at DurableHuman.com/BMICalculator.

Once you know your BMI, staying within your healthy range depends on your physical activity and what you eat. As the CDC Division of Nutrition, Physical Activity, and Obesity states on its website:

> *To remain in balance and maintain your body weight, the calories consumed (from foods) must be balanced by the calories used (in normal body functions, daily activities, and exercise).*

To calculate the foods and exercise you need to drive your body in a durable direction, visit DurableHuman.com/SuperTracker.

If your BMI is on the high side (a BMI over 25 is considered overweight), your blood sugar levels may also be higher and you could already be in a state of pre-diabetes.[84] If you don't do anything about it, there's a good chance you'll have full-blown type 2 diabetes within ten years.[85]

On the flip side, if you have a high BMI, the American Diabetes Association says you can control your health destiny by taking the durable steps we've already covered:

- Stay within your BMI.
- Eat foods on which our species evolved.
- Be physically active.

If you're at especially high risk for diabetes (your BMI is higher, you're over forty-five years old, don't exercise, have high blood pressure and a few other factors), you can seize the Triple Crown with the CDC's National Diabetes Prevention Program. Participants spend a year meeting in small groups with a coach who helps them eat healthier, move more, and improve "problem-solving and coping skills."

"It's actually the intervention that has the most evidence behind it," reports Ann Albright of the CDC Division of Diabetes Translation. Over five years of research, those who followed the program cut their risk of developing type 2 diabetes by nearly sixty percent.[86]

But, because we humans evolved outdoors, we need something else besides food to shine with durability.

Sun and Bones

Like many other American boys his age, fifteen-year-old Justin (not his real name) liked to play video games more than sports. That was, until he began to notice his knees hurt when he'd get up from the couch.[87]

X-rays revealed Justin had hairline fractures in both shinbones. He also had the early signs of rickets,[88] a condition caused by a chronic lack of vitamin D.

In the United States and Canada, through interventions such as vitamin D-fortified milk and infant vitamin supplements, rickets had been largely eradicated—until recently, when the disease began to creep back.[89]

"Vitamin D deficiency or nutritional rickets can show up in several ways. If the problem starts early, kids' growth may be severely stunted. The arms or legs may not grow straight, or bones may be weak and easily broken," explains Ellen Raney, a pediatrician at Shriners Hospitals for Children in Portland, Oregon.[90]

Vitamin D helps our bodies absorb the calcium and phosphorus which we need for healthy bones, nerves, muscles, and cellular activities.

Women lacking vitamin D have a greater chance of osteoporosis, a disease leading to brittle bones and fractures, especially of the hips and spine.[91]

Besides the cup of "dairy" shown on ChooseMyPlate, not many foods contain vitamin D, except for the flesh of salmon and some fatty fish. In foods labeled "fortified" with vitamin D, the vitamin was added.

Luckily, you are a human animal and don't need to rely solely on your diet to get enough vitamin D. Your body makes it for you when you expose your skin to the sun.[92]

The amount of the vitamin your body produces depends on many factors, including the season, time of day, cloud cover, air quality, skin pigmentation, and what you eat. (Note that sitting in the sun behind a windowpane doesn't work.)

By the way, even if your skin has a lot of pigment—your heritage is African, for instance—you still produce vitamin D.

As for how much sun you need, according to Michael Holwick, M.D., writing in the *American Journal of Clinical Nutrition*:

Usually, five to ten minutes of exposure of the arms and legs or the hands, arms, and face, two to three times per week and increased dietary and supplemental vitamin D intakes are reasonable approaches to guarantee vitamin D sufficiency.[93]

Five to ten minutes of direct sunlight isn't even quite long enough to pinken lighter-toned skin, yet even this limited exposure has prompted statements of concern, including the American Academy of Dermatology's "Don't Seek the Sun: Top Reasons to Get Vitamin D from Your Diet."[94]

The American Academy of Dermatology (AAD) and Skin Cancer Foundation both worry that exposing unprotected skin to the ultraviolet light of sunshine makes a person prone to skin cancer and premature aging of the skin.[95]

In this situation, you need to weigh the pros and cons for yourself, but you might consider the advice of Dr. Holwick, a member of the AAD. He says to go ahead and have the five or ten minutes two or three days a week, then, "after this exposure, application of a sunscreen of Sun Protection Factor (SPF) 15 or higher is recommended to prevent the damaging effects of chronic excessive exposure to sunlight."

As for Justin—with more exercise, sunshine, and vitamin D—his shin splints slowly healed.

By the way, when you get sun, exercise, and eat nutritious food, you're also increasing the durability of all the little critters who call you Home.

Caring for Your Microbiome

Imagine, if you would, a towering oak. Although it looks alone, it actually plays host to a menagerie. Hundreds of creatures live in the tree—from caterpillars, ants, and crawly things, to squirrels, birds, and other more obvious wildlife.

You also have a band of hidden inhabitants. But, rather than a few hundred, there are one hundred trillion microscopic creatures living in and on your body.

The invisible legions of bacteria, fungi, and viruses—known collectively as your microbiome—is as unique to you as your fingerprint. You probably have one band of tiny beasties on your right hand and another on your left.[96]

You need your microbiome as much as it needs you. Scientists are just beginning to understand how the tiny microbes within you help digest food, express genes, moderate your immune system, and perform a yet-to-be determined number of other jobs.

You can see how the microbiome works in a fascinating video that animator Ben Arthur created for NPR[97] at DurableHuman.com/MicrobiomeMovie.

Your microbiome is with you from the start.

When a human baby travels through the mother's birth canal, she inoculates him or her with her own helpful microbes. Even before that, her microbiome helps the fetus establish a healthy brain and digestive system. (Breast milk also transfers helpful microbes.)

Researchers worry that babies born by Cesarean section may be missing out because they aren't properly "infected." That's why some C-section babies are being inoculated with their mothers' bacteria immediately after birth.[98]

Since our species and our microbes evolved together, they thrive on the same foods we do.[99] So, shifting from the natural way of eating to a diet of artificial and highly processed foods is a shock to our systems and threatens our legions of micro-organisms.

Take the puzzling conundrum that artificial sweeteners could actually make some people *gain* weight. Researchers suspect the chemicals somehow hurt the microbiome.[100] This makes sense considering the sweeteners are made in a laboratory and aren't something with which we evolved. The CDC even hedges its support for government-approved artificial sweeteners, mentioning in the dietary guidelines:

> *It should be noted that replacing added sugars with high-intensity sweeteners may reduce calorie intake in the short-term, yet questions remain about their effectiveness as a long-term weight management strategy.*

Scientists have also observed that fried foods can upset the creatures inside your gut. Researchers speculate that the food disrupts the feedback loop between the creatures and your brain that signals you've had enough to eat.

"We should be aware that on a high-fat (and high-carbohydrate) diet, balance in the intestinal microbiota and gut-brain communication—which was developing over thousands and thousands of years in humans and animals—has been interrupted by the introduction of modified foods. This leads to the confused brain and inappropriate satiety feedback and results in obesity," according to University of Georgia neuroanatomy researcher Krzysztof Czaja.[101]

The microbiome's impact on health is profound, according to Jeff Leach, founder of The American Gut Project. Leach is collecting stool samples from people all over the U.S., curious to find out exactly how the microbiome is affected, not only by diet, but lots of other factors, including age, whether you have kids or pets, and even where you live.

While scientists rush to learn more, the best bet for keeping your microbiome healthy is to try and avoid machine- and lab-made fare and to eat mainly what you and your crew evolved on: foods that grow from the earth and in the ocean. It also may help you maintain a normal BMI. "A healthy diet encourages microbes associated with leanness to become incorporated into the gut," reports obesity researcher Jeffrey Gordon of the Washington University School of Medicine.[102]

But something else besides food is causing havoc for our microbiomes: our lab-made antibacterial soaps and cleaners. "We are causing extensive damage. It's like an atomic bomb in our body," says Maria Gloria Dominguez-Bello, a microbiologist from the University of Puerto Rico.[103] She is so convinced antiseptic consumer products are hurting the modern microbiome, she's gone to the Amazon to study the intestinal workings of members of primitive societies to find out what a healthy microbiome is supposed to look like.

Durable Human Designs for Your Microbiome

The irony is, although detergents and soaps with antibacterial agents may cost more, they don't necessarily work any better than those without. According to the CDC:

> *To date, studies have shown that there is no added health benefit for consumers (this does not include professionals in the healthcare setting) using soaps [including household cleaners] containing antibacterial ingredients compared with using plain soap.[104]*

But how can you clean your hands without antiseptics? As the CDC puts it,

> *Washing hands with soap and water is the best way to reduce the number of germs on them in most situations.*

There are even official U.S. government guidelines for this simple Jewel 1 skill:

- Wet hands with clean, running water (warm or cold), turn off the tap, and apply soap.
- Rub hands together to create lather, then scrub your fingers and under your nails for at least twenty seconds (long enough to hum "Happy Birthday" twice).
- Rinse hands well under clean, running water.
- Dry with a clean towel or allow hands to air dry.

When soap and water is not available, the CDC says hand sanitizer is useful, with these caveats:

- Check the label. Unless the product is 60 percent alcohol, it may not offer effective germ protection.
- Alcohol-based hand sanitizers don't eliminate all germs, so some may remain on your hands even after using.
- Follow product directions carefully:
  - Apply only the amount recommended (usually one squirt).
  - Apply first in the palm of one hand.
  - Rub evenly over both hands until dry.
- Hand sanitizers don't remove dirt or grease, so washing greasy hands with soap and water is preferable.

There is no question antibiotic medicine has contributed mightily to the ongoing durability of our species. Ironically, though, in part because we have so misused and overused the drugs, some bacteria have become resistant to antibiotics' effects. So you don't contribute to the problem, take antibiotic medication exactly as prescribed and only when necessary.

CHAPTER 5:
PAY ATTENTION

We had time. Now we have no time. Where did it go?

Lewis Carroll, from *Through the Looking Glass*

Not long ago, when four out of five American adults weighed about right for their heights, people sat down for something called the Dinner Hour and would linger that long over just one meal.

Microsoft founder Bill Gates recalls fondly how he'd sit around the dinner table with his parents: "It was a rich environment in which to learn."[105]

Today, it takes the average U.S. resident a total of about an hour to eat all three meals plus snacks. Four percent of Americans report they *never eat at all.*[106]

I asked Laura Wronski of the U.S. Bureau of Labor Statistics to explain how people could fill out the Time Use Survey yet never eat.

"Our time-use estimates do not capture simultaneous activities," she told me in an email. "So if someone says he was watching TV while eating dinner, we ask him to break out the time spent in each activity or to only report the primary activity. In that case, his primary activity was watching TV."[107]

So, not only do we spend less time eating, we don't pay attention when we do.

What you don't want to hear is this:

> *My mom is always on the iPad at dinner. She's always "just*
> *checking." I really wish she would just talk.*

Catherine Steiner-Adair, a Harvard clinical psychologist, collected that comment when she interviewed hundreds of American kids between the ages of eleven and eighteen. "It feels like all you [adults] care about is your phone," one child told her.

I saw it in my own parenting. As my youngest child grew and personal technology became more enticing, I became less attentive. Social media consumed more and more of my time. I became comfortable as hours would sometimes slip by and he'd be on one screen and I'd be on mine.

This subtle slide toward inattention has left kids "mad, sad, and lonely," reports Steiner-Adair. Because their kids can't catch their eyes and ears, parents are missing out on what she calls "the mini-moments of childhood."[108]

"Kids give up on their parents and tech becomes the *de facto* go-to parent," Steiner-Adair reported at the 2013 Family Online Safety Institute annual conference. She describes such "relationship fatigue" in her book, *The Big Disconnect: Protecting Childhood and Family Relationships in the Digital Age.*[109]

The Corrosion of Neglect

Decades into the digital age, scientists are taking cues from adults who grew up in Romanian orphanages during the 1980s and 90s. As children, they had spent months alone in their cribs with virtually no physical affection or attention from adults.

Today these people not only struggle with long-term mental and emotional problems, their brains are physically smaller. "We found a dramatic reduction in what's referred to as grey matter and in white matter," says Charles Nelson, a professor of pediatrics at Harvard Medical School and Boston Children's Hospital. "Neglect is awful for the brain. The wiring of the brain goes awry."[110] (Grey matter is mainly for thought processing, while white matter is more structural and is used to transmit nerve impulses.)

Researchers from Sweden's Karolinska Institute medical university found out what happens when parents don't notice their teens' "mini moments." Apparently, one out of every three Swedish teenagers falls into an "invisible group" at special risk for psychiatric problems. They spend an excessive amount of time on screen-based media, get little exercise, and not enough sleep. Yet, even with this triple whammy, they fly under their parents' radar.

"While parents are likely to notice if a child is using drugs or getting drunk," say the researchers, "they may easily overlook adolescents engaging in unobtrusive behaviors, such as watching too much TV, not playing sports, or sleeping too little."[111]

As captivated as they may be, we do children no favors by always leaving them to their devices.

Doctors in Korea write of a fifteen-year-old who, from the time he was five years old, "intensively" watched TV, played video games, and was on the web. Now, they say, he has "digital dementia" and can't even remember the six-digit code to get into his house.

"Overuse of smartphones and game devices hampers the balanced development of the brain," researcher Byun Gi-won of the Balanced Brain Center in Seoul, South Korea, reported in a United Press International news story.[112]

On the other hand, in their book *Nurture Shock: New Thinking About Children*, Po Bronson and Ashley Merryman cite compelling evidence of how, when a loving person gives a babbling baby a pat of encouragement, it can turbo-charge the baby's growing vocabulary.[113]

We underestimate the power that touch, eye contact, and conversation have on human beings. These are reasons beyond safety that checking email while bathing your toddler is not a wise idea.

Even when they become champion coders or sovereigns of social media, kids still need physical affection and the guidance of caring adults. "Relationship is hugely important," declares Justin Patchin, a criminal justice professor and co-director of the Cyberbullying Research Center.[114]

The art of conversation is a critical component in normal child development. In her work helping children hear through cochlear implants, Chicago pediatric surgeon Dana Suskind noticed that language ability improved quickly in some of her implanted patients, but not in others. She discovered that, among patients who didn't improve, there was little conversation at home.

Dr. Suskind earned at least two jewels of the Triple Crown when her curiosity and compassion led her on a quest. She set out to tell parents that more conversation is crucial—especially in low-income households where studies show fewer words are spoken. Where at-home banter has increased, Suskind has seen great improvements in children's language skills: "You can almost look into their eyes and see neural connections happening."[115]

The Meaning of Efficient

The word *efficient* has a special meaning when it comes to human beings.

In *The Seven Habits of Highly Effective People*, Stephen Covey writes that machines are considered efficient when they churn out the most work in the least amount of time. But, Covey says, to be efficient with people you need to do the opposite: stop what you're doing and listen.

When you were growing up, your parents probably weren't as distracted as you are now. Chances are more likely that when you talked, they listened. Today's kids—or anyone seeking your solace and advice—still need that same kind of undivided attention.

To be durable is to know you are entering (or are in) a state of pre-occupation. When desktop computers were the only game in town, I imagined a sign above my desk that would read:

> ***Turn Around When They Come Around.***

Though we're mobile now—with tablets, laptops, and phones—the spirit of the message still applies.

Sherry Turkle is the director of the Initiative on Technology and Self at the Massachusetts Institute of Technology (MIT). Her view as an author is that personal digital devices interfere with human relationships, yet she says, "This is not a moment to reject technology, but to find ourselves."[116]

The Pinch of Generosity

One of your greatest assets as a human being is the capacity to be generous, the meaning of which can be confusing.

Giving that old, stained coat to a homeless shelter may count as generosity, but it can be a relief to pitch it. True generosity hurts, just a little.

As philosopher C.S. Lewis mused:

> ***If our charities do not at all pinch or hamper us, I should say they are too small.***[117]

It *pinches* not to check your phone when you want to.

I remember one rainy Saturday morning, I got up early to have lots of uninterrupted time to put the finishing touches on this book. I was about to dig in when my husband suggested we go out to get breakfast. Though it pinched to say yes, I felt better knowing I was exercising my generosity muscle.

And, get this: being generous creates an amazing feedback loop in your mind that makes *you* happier. According to Richard Davidson, founder of the Center for Healthy Minds at the University of Wisconsin-Madison, "The most effective strategy for changing specific circuits in the brain associated with well-being is generosity."[118]

If you are a durable parent or caregiver, your decisions may be different from the crowd's. Out to dinner with a restless five-year-old, you may be the only one in the room playing Hangman instead of handing over your phone.

Once little kids get their hands on those cool, shiny objects, it can be agonizing after that to *just say no*. That's why waiting a while to introduce your child to technology can save you years of strife. As one dad told me, "The worst thing I ever did was let my two-year-old get her hands on my iPad."

Last Generation, B.C.

If you are in your twenties or older, consider yourself lucky. You are part of the Last Generation, B.C.—the vanishing cohort of humans who grew up Before Cellphones. As a kid, you were wild and unplugged. You relied mostly on yourself to reason through problems. When you were fidgety, your mom or dad had no handy digital device to entertain you. Sometimes you sat minutes on end in a doctor's office with only your thoughts and some tattered magazines. Enduring short bouts of frustration was one way you naturally learned to be durable.

In *The Durable Human Manifesto*, I write about how Steve Jobs and Steve Wozniak teamed up to create the first personal computer, asking:

> *One wonders what might have happened if the Steves were born today. Would the flicker of a parent's smartphone usurp young Jobs's wandering thoughts? Would video games devour little Woz's time to tinker?*

Durable Parenting in the Digital Age

The perception exists that babies today are "born digital"—as if they arrive already knowing how to code. But today's newborns are just like those who came before them—as wild and untethered as the squirrels in the trees. Only later will a child plug in to the digital world. Until then, early childhood is the only time in a person's life he or she has totally unfettered time to discover his or her one-of-a-kind interests and aptitudes.

The pressure is on, though, to close a child's wild human window. But there's an opportunity cost to curtailing a child's process of discovery. By always handing over your tablet or giving her an electric trike that does the peddling, she may never fully know her *own* operating system and what makes *herself* tick.

When you were growing up, you had plenty of time to be wild. But, though today's kids will never know a pre-digital world, they still deserve *their* own wild time, not only to get to know themselves, but to increase our species' chance of ongoing relevance.

To enrich the web of neural connections inside their brains, little kids need to explore the world with *all* their senses, not just those associated with wiping a finger across a screen.

As I write in *The Manifesto:*

Today's parents' sacred trust is to jealously guard their children's chance to be wild. To give them time, not to take it away.

This is not to say that thoughtfully using a device with your child cannot be useful. "If parents and educators are using media intentionally and recognize certain sources as a prompt for conversation and real social interaction, then it can be harnessed to truly improve language development and literacy. But we have to use it intentionally," says Lisa Guernsey, director of the Learning Technologies Project at the non-profit New America.[119]

Yet, even if parents facilitate, new evidence shows that exposure to electronic screened devices should be limited in very young children.

"Though these screens look so simple and babies are able to just sort of zip around a touch screen no problem, it's actually not as easy as it looks when we really closely measure it," reports Rebecca Barr, a Georgetown University researcher who studies how toddlers interact with technology.[120]

Whether e-book, touch screen, computer, or television, Barr says, "All of these sorts of media add symbols, and symbols are very difficult for toddlers to understand." As she continues, "When they learn that information from the symbol and then they come out into the real world, we see a deficit. So we see less learning from them than from a face-to-face interaction."

According to the American Academy of Pediatrics (AAP), children age two and under should avoid TV and entertainment media. All other young people are advised to use media thoughtfully. Realizing what a utility the Internet has become for things like homework, the AAP suggests that when kids use electronics simply for entertainment, parents should consider setting a time limit of two hours.

Kids also need guidance about when to use those hours.

"Beware of the forbidden fruit syndrome," warns Michael Rich, a pediatrician and founder of Children's Hospital Boston Center on Media and Child Health. As Dr. Rich explained to me, strict restrictions can backfire. "Kids will come home from school and the first thing they do is go and get their two hours of TV or tablet or video game time. They're using their best time—the time when they are the sharpest and full of the most energy—to do a default activity, rather than the important activities of their lives."[121]

Parents need to watch out for whether kids' tech use, as Dr. Rich says, "excludes or displaces other aspects that are necessary for their health and development, such as sleep, spending time with family, outdoor play, physical play."[122]

The whole idea, in Dr. Rich's view, is to:

Build a menu of diversity which makes them a richer, fuller person.

Your kids actually want you to be there as they learn technology, just as when you taught them to tie their shoes. According to iKeepSafe.org, two out of three kids between ages eight and twelve consider their parents tech experts, as does one out of five teenagers.

According to a 2016 survey by the Pew Research Center, more than half of parents have limited when their teenagers can go online and have withdrawn cellphone or Internet privileges at one time or another.[123]

Durable parents know they can't be passive about their kids' digital existence. They become familiar with the devices their kids use and set up age-appropriate parental controls. They sit with their children to work out the technology ground rules, perhaps by using The Smart

Talk. Designed by the National Parent Teacher Association, the interactive tool allows you and your child to draw up a customized tech use agreement that covers areas including texting, posting photos, online activities, and who has responsibility for phones and other devices.

The PTA has certainly achieved the Triple Crown with The Smart Talk, but the design only covers the digital aspects of your child's life. Your attention is needed in all the other aspects, too. Luckily, though, because you have the perspective borne of growing up without the aid of wireless devices, you're in the best position to help reverse what Dr. Rich describes as "trading connectivity for connectedness."

There is no question it takes gumption—and often ingenuity—to step in and interrupt a child's reverie, but in doing so, know you are educating her or him on some aspect of the Triple Crown.

A middle school math teacher friend of mine noticed how some of her students were frittering away their free time, constantly chatting about the Kardashians. But, rather than shutting that down, she used her ingenuity to start a lunchtime knitting club. Now, the kids have a new Jewel 1 self-reliance skill and talk just as much about yarn and purling as they do about Kim and Khloe. They also understand the empowering, creative feeling of *making something*.

Club members' efforts were amplified when they donated squares they knitted to Warm Up America, a charity which made them into a blanket and gave it to someone in need.

We do kids the ultimate service when we teach them to fish, rather than fishing for them.

A college classmate of mine who's now a Franciscan friar also taught middle schoolers. The school is in Camden, New Jersey—right next door to what he dubbed "the nation's most depressing park." He wanted his students to know how to solve their own neighborhood problems, so he started an after-school class in civic engagement.

After the kids chose the park as their community-improvement project, they wrote letters and met with the appropriate local, state and congressional officials. Within two years, the park was fully restored, along with a full-sized baseball field. In the process, what came to be known as the Student Leaders' Von Nieda Park Task Force also convinced officials to spend millions of dollars to fix a sewer system that had periodically flooded neighborhood basements and streets for decades.[124]

Now the kids from Camden teach other students how to solve their own problems. Several Student Leaders have gone on to receive high school and college scholarships, at least in part because of their durability-building community work.

Durable Human Designs for Paying Better Attention

Mealtime may be the only time all day family members can sit down together. But whether breakfast, lunch, or dinner, bringing technology to the table can get in the way of the second jewel of the Triple Crown: high-touch, heart-to-heart relationships.

For our family, I place a basket just out of reach of the table. Before sitting down, anyone with a wireless device places it on silent and pops it into the basket.

On holidays, visiting devices also get to have their own fun in the gadget basket.

Other ways to promote mealtime interaction:

- If you are the cook, rather than doling out food onto each plate, use serving bowls instead. You will have more time to sit down and everyone can practice sharing and cooperation.

- Encourage others to share in the cooking and cleanup. They can chat while brushing up on Jewel 1—their skills of self-reliance.
- After dinner, if everyone packs his or her own lunch for the next day, not only will it add to your time together, it will reduce stress in the morning.

People in Denmark cherish a time they call *hygge*, when family members leave their worries and agendas behind. "It is a light-hearted, balanced interaction that is focused on enjoying the moment, the food, and the company," writes Jessica Alexander and her Danish husband in *The Danish Way of Parenting: A Guide to Raising the Happiest Kids in the World*. (They have two of their own.)

"By dedicating specific time to *hygge* we can create a safe space for families and friends to be together without stress. However, it takes everyone wanting this and working together to achieve it," Alexander advises.[125]

Carving out no-pressure time together is certainly a great way to build a durable family, but there will come times when family members need to hash things out—whether to address simmering feuds, dole out chores, or acknowledge an elephant in the living room.

For those times, my family uses a talking stick, which Wikipedia terms "an instrument of aboriginal democracy." Also known as a speaker's staff, the talking stick is used by many indigenous peoples, especially native tribes on the northwest coast of North America.

The way it works is that the person holding the stick is the only member of the group who is permitted to speak. The stick is passed around so, eventually, everyone in the group has a chance to be heard. "Especially those who may be shy," says Wikipedia. "Consensus can force the stick to move along to assure that the 'long winded' don't dominate the discussion. The person holding the stick may allow others to inter-ject." (Author's note: the talking stick works best in combination with the gadget basket.)

When it's time for meetings of only a few relatives—such as taking your pre-teen with you to lunch with Great Aunt Sally—kids are eager to pull out their devices. As you ponder whether to ask them not to, keep in mind that in this world of copying and sharing, you and your child are about to have a one-of-a-kind, never-to-be-repeated oppor-tunity to learn some family history.

It is a challenge to be a durable parent in the digital world. You need stamina to pay attention to your loved ones' needs in the daytime—and all through the night.

CHAPTER 6:
SEEK SLEEP AND SANCTUARY

O sleep, O gentle sleep, Nature's soft nurse, how have I frighted thee, that thou no more wilt weigh my eyelids down and steep my senses in forgetfulness?

William Shakespeare, from *Henry IV*

The colors of the stained glass windows play on the granite pillars as my teenaged son sits quietly beside me. Although he may not be listening to what happens on the altar, he's alone with his thoughts, and this may be the only waking hour all week he does not have a phone in his hand.

According to Merriam-Webster, the word *sanctuary* means "a place of refuge and protection." A church is one kind of sanctuary—a quiet place to think through the complicated affairs of the day and have a chance "to plant our own dream blossoms," as Anne Morrow Lindbergh writes in *Gift from the Sea*.

But having space in your life to *do nothing* is a vanishing commodity. The realm of silence was once "the context of thought, conversation, and general existence, but is now as rare as a virgin forest," says Maggie Jackson in her book, *Distracted: The Erosion of Attention and the Coming Dark Age*.

Remember the Danish practice of *hygge?* Author Jessica Alexander describes it as "a shelter from the outside world."

To be durable is to actively seek sanctuary.

My cousin used the word after she brought home a new puppy. With three kids under age ten, friends and family warned her that adding a dog to the mix might be too much to manage. But, as she later told me, "When I take her out, we're alone. I hear the birds and can hear myself think. Do you think I can ever do that inside the house?"

As human animals, we bloom in the breeze and sunshine. As naturalist and thinker Martin Ogle told an audience of nature educators,

There are a lot of questions that being outdoors helps answer.

Dogs and breezes notwithstanding, trying to find peace and quiet during the day can be daunting. Luckily, your body has a marvelous way to help you recover from being blasted with non-stop input, action, and information: the biological sanctuary of sleep.

Sleep Services

Your brain during sleep is like an old-fashioned file clerk, neatly sliding what you learned during the day into long-term storage. "It's kind of like your brain is rehearsing stuff without you knowing, while you're asleep," reports neuroscientist Penelope Lewis in *The Secret World of Sleep: The Surprising Science of the Mind at Rest.*

Sleep also does to the brain what a dishwasher does to dishes.[126] While you sleep, harmful waste products that have built up during the day are flushed away, according to researchers at the University of Rochester.[127] You want your cerebral dishwasher to have a chance to work because some waste products are similar to the toxins found in the neural tangles of Alzheimer's disease.[128]

During sleep, your body also does maintenance, such as building up muscle mass and repairing damaged cells. It's a sweet deal, really. All you need to do is conk out.

The blissful feeling of falling asleep happens when your body produces more of the protein prolactin. "Prolactin creates a feeling of security, quietness, and peace. And it is intimately, and biologically, tied to the dark," according to Clark Strand, author of *Waking Up to the Dark: Ancient Wisdom for a Sleepless Age*.[129]

Our body chemistry is set up and organized around a twenty-four-hour clock, according to Michael Twery, director of the National Institutes of Health (NIH) National Center on Sleep Disorders Research: "Not getting enough sleep, or sleeping irregularly, may lead to the erosion of our health, not only in our minds, but also in tissues throughout the body—our liver, our heart, our fat cells, the insulin-secreting cells, and many others."[130]

Disrupted sleep can also disrupt relationships. According to a California study, couples found it harder to get along after only one night's unsettled sleep.[131]

The jet-lagged feeling of sleep deprivation wreaks havoc on your willpower, so you're more likely to grab for that candy bar or pack of cigarettes[132] or to thumb compulsively through Facebook.

Without enough sleep, it's harder for your body to defend itself. After a single sleepless night, the effectiveness of your immune system can drop by as much as 25 percent. Skimp on sleep and you're twice as likely to catch a cold.[133]

But wait, there's much more: "People who are sleeping less than six hours a night are at risk for more cardiovascular events, are more likely to develop diabetes, and are more likely to die sooner," says University of California at San Francisco research psychologist Aric Prather.[134]

The course of human development has always been governed by the circadian experience of light and darkness. But here in the digital age, we're no longer in sync with the sun. As I write in *The Manifesto*, the only windows some of us see are made by Microsoft.

Yet, sleep is as important as ever, if only to clear the way for you to think and do. "The quality of your sleep determines the quality of being awake," circadian neuroscientist Russell Foster said in a TED talk: "Those synapses that are strengthened for creativity are strengthened when we sleep."

The key to restful slumber is to follow, or at least imitate, a circadian rhythm. "Having a rhythmicity to sleep and wake patterns is crucial to having healthy sleep," affirms the University of Washington Medicine Sleep Center's Nathaniel Watson.[135]

But there's a lot of anxiety surrounding exactly how much sleep we need.

To settle the question, researchers from UCLA's Semel Institute of Neuroscience and Human Behavior visited three far-flung pre-industrial cultures. Surprisingly, in each of them, people tended to hang around the fire long after nightfall and sleep an average of only six-and-a-half hours per night, with no apparent untoward effects.[136]

But whether we get six-and-a-half or the seven-to-eight hours per night recommended by the CDC, the way we use our devices can throw a wrench into our attempts.

If you happen to be among the 90 percent of Americans who look at a phone or tablet within an hour of wanting to sleep, know that those final peeks put the brakes on rising levels of your go-to-sleep hormone, melatonin.[137]

Little lights in your sleeping space don't help either.

When you open your eyes in the night and see the tiny indicator light on your smoke alarm, the "photons [tiny particles of light] cue the brain to be awake," says Dan Siegel of the UCLA Mindful Awareness Research Center.[138] I put a Post-it® note over the piercing light of my bedroom thermostat.

Devices you carry into your bedroom can be even more disruptive. Your phone is a funnel for texts, notifications, and other things that can go beep in the night.

Durable Human Designs for Sleeping Well

Most of these solid sleep suggestions come from the American Academy of Sleep Medicine:

- Try to go to bed and get up around the same time each day.
- Wind down with a quiet activity like reading—on paper or a device that doesn't emit blue light (which interferes with melatonin production).
- Remember that caffeine and alcohol are sleep disrupters.
- Try not to go to bed hungry or right after a big meal.
- Besides being dark and quiet, your sleeping space should be on the cooler side—between 60 and 67 degrees Fahrenheit.
- So you don't hear every little ping, charge your phone and tablet well away from your bed, such as in a hallway or bathroom.

That last item will take forethought and willpower and most likely is going to *pinch*. But we must be vigilant to keep our phones away from our sleeping space, according to Daniel Lewin, psychologist and sleep specialist at Children's National Health System. Otherwise, he says, "If they're in the bedroom, shut them down on a mode where they're not going to disrupt our sleep or tempt us."[139]

Wait a minute, you might be thinking. *If you're suggesting I sleep without my phone, I can't because I need it to wake up in the morning.*

A good old alarm clock can solve that problem. (If it's a digital clock, be sure to angle the bright numbers on its face away from yours.)

After I wrote a post on this topic,[140] a thoughtful reader shared his sleep strategy, which involves a helpful app:

> *It sounds like a nice Tibetan chime, at first very softly and then progressively louder. This is pleasing, but more importantly, wakes me up without waking my wife. Normally, I would charge [the phone] in the kitchen, which is what I do on the (sadly few) days when I don't need an alarm. Also, I have the beeps turned off, use "do not disturb" mode, and silence everything but the alarm clock at night.*

Later, he wrote back:

> *Another solution just occurred to me that is so obvious I can't believe I didn't think of it before: I can take one of our old, retired iPhones, disable everything I can and leave off all of those tempting apps, and use it for nothing but running that alarm clock app.*

That, my friends, is durable human design.

Meanwhile, the quality of kids' sleep is going downhill fast—and their parents are pushing the sled.

Kids, Sleep, and Sanctuary

It was way back in 1998 that kids as young as ten first reported a sense of information overload.[141] Flash forward to today and the time the average elementary school kid spends on screens has ballooned to six hours a day, while teens spend almost nine.[142] More than one in every ten kids worry they're addicted to or obsessed with technology.[143]

As it is for you, a child's bedroom may be his or her only sanctuary—a place to take a deep breath and think things through.

Kids also need sleep for their brains to grow and develop normally. Sleep is "essential to making just-learned information consolidate, or stick in memory," according to the publisher of *The Dana Guide to Brain Health*.[144] That means, if a child doesn't sleep well, the answers may not be there for the test the next day.

A large British study also showed that seven-year-olds who had unpredictable and irregular sleep schedules tended to be more impulsive and have other behavioral problems.[145]

On the other hand, when German researchers studied a group of seven-year-olds, those who'd had good sleep habits since toddlerhood performed better in the classroom.[146]

Kids need more sleep than adults do. Infants usually sleep for twelve hours at a stretch, plus take naps. By the time children are twelve and naps are over, they still need upwards of eleven hours of sleep a day.

Teens are supposed to get nine hours of sleep, but the National Sleep Foundation reports that a mere 15 percent manage to get even eight hours on a school night.[147]

Like everything else, a child's sleep habits begin at home—a worrisome thought considering one in every three kids under age three is allowed a TV or other type of screen in the bedroom, which some parents mistakenly believe enhances sleep.[148]

"There is some real concern here because we know that TV is not calming, in fact it increases bedtime resistance and reduces the quality of sleep. So, kids are getting less quality and quantity of sleep, which is really important for their growing bodies and their growing brains," observes Ari Brown of the American Academy of Pediatrics (AAP).[149]

Phones and tablets in a child's bedroom are even more disruptive than TV and computer displays, not only because of pings in the night, but because it's so tempting to text and play games beyond Lights Out.

In a major study of fourth and seventh graders, kids who had phones in the bedroom slept significantly less each night than kids without. The kids themselves reported feeling more tired during the day than kids without phones in their bedrooms.[150]

AAP members are supposed to ask these questions when kids come in for a checkup:[151]

> *How much recreational screen time does your child or teenager consume daily?*

> *Is there a television set or Internet-connected device in the child's bedroom?*

Over the past decade, the diagnosis of ADHD has nearly doubled among kids under eighteen.[152] In his book *What Causes ADHD?*, psychiatrist Joel Nigg has developed an "attention hygiene checklist"[153] with questions about whether the child goes out to play or has a frenetic home life. But right at the top is this one:

> *Is the child getting eight to ten hours of sleep a night?*

The American Academy of Pediatrics doesn't mince words about kids, tech, and sleep:

> *Keep the TV set and Internet-connected electronic devices out of the child's bedroom.*

Bedtimes for kids should roughly follow the cycles of the sun.[154] As we've seen, if kids have a consistent, natural sleep rhythm, they learn better, they're healthier, and they have better control of their own behavior.

Durable Human Designs to Help Kids Sleep Well

Most of these tips are from the National Sleep Foundation:[155]

For young children

- A child's sleeping space should be quiet and comfortable with little or no light.
- Establish a regular bedtime and stick to it every night, including weekends.
- Help younger kids relax before bedtime with low-excitement activities such as eating a light snack, taking a bath, brushing teeth, putting on pajamas, and reading a physical book.
- Arrange your home so media devices like computers and game consoles are away from the sleeping area.
- Kids should stop playing video games and using digital devices at least an hour before bedtime.

For kids under age ten, books can help teach the importance of restful sleep. Standouts are *The Quiet Book* by Deborah Underwood. Watercolor bunnies and bears deliver calming messages such as, "Quiet can be sweet and cozy, and can most definitely help you fall asleep."

Animals Need ZZZ's, Too, by Patricia Britz, teaches healthy sleep practices as it depicts the real-life sleep behavior of koalas, penguins, horses, and other animals.

Your powerful sense of touch calms and nurtures a child when you cuddle up to read.

For older kids

To encourage teens to get more sleep, remind them that sleep-deprived people are more likely to:

• Break out in pimples
• Put on weight
• Fall asleep behind the wheel

Overall

To instill a lifetime of durable sleep habits:

• During babyhood: design a quiet, peaceful sleep environment where baby can sleep and wake up naturally.
• For toddlers: set a consistent bedtime, then stick with it.
• When it's time for school: continue to ensure a consistent bedtime and that the sleep environment is cool, quiet, dark, and without electronics.
• Throughout the school years: continue to make sure your kids don't have computers, cellphones, and other digital devices in the bedroom when it's time to sleep.

And don't forget those gifts of alarm clocks and watches.

Thankfully, at least one tech company has redesigned a personal digital device to encourage sensible sleep habits and life balance. With the Amazon Fire Kids Edition, kids can read and play with many pre-screened, age-appropriate books and activities. Then, after an amount of time designated by the caregiver, the machine displays a friendly goodbye message and shuts down, gently ushering kids to do other things.

But getting better sleep isn't the only reason not to get too cozy with your devices.

CHAPTER 7:

COME TO YOUR SENSES

The faintness of the stars, the freshness of the morning, the dewdrop of the flower, speaks to me.

Chief Dan George, from his poem "My Heart Soars"

Out with my dog on a warm spring morning, I step off the path and up to a magnolia blossom perched on the end of a long branch. The luscious fragrance strikes me even before I can sniff, as dew drops dapple my nose with their tiny, cool shower.

It feels so darned good to be human—and not only when you stop to smell the flowers.

"Magic happens when humans touch" are the words in *The Manifesto:*

> *Your fingers are veritable magic wands. If it were possible to bottle a hug, it could be sold as a combination muscle relaxant, tranquilizer, and love potion.*

That we can communicate merely through eye contact is another of our remarkable abilities. "We are hardwired to be constantly scanning others' [faces] to see if they're safe," says psychologist Ron Siegel of Harvard Medical School.[156]

Thankfully, our senses can also adapt. Those who lose their ability to see, for instance, develop more acute hearing and can amazingly learn to read with their fingertips.

Even now, deep into the digital age, our survival still depends on smelling the smoke, hearing the ambulance, and sensing other warning signs.

But, even though our senses are so central to our existence, we typically pay them no mind. We also fail to realize how our senses can be inadvertently damaged by our devices.

Our family was once at a wedding reception having dinner as a band performed softly in the background. But when I nudged my son, Brian, that they were playing one of my favorite songs, he looked concerned. "Mom," he said. "I can't really hear the music."

Taken aback his hearing could possibly be worse than mine, I thought for a moment, then asked him, "Do you listen to music at work?"

"Yes," he answered. "To drown out other sounds so I can concentrate."

Can You Hear Me Later?

When the Sony Walkman was introduced in 1980, music was liberated. Suddenly, we could listen to whatever, wherever we wanted. The headphones allowed a private listening experience we didn't have to share with anyone else.

Twenty-one years later, the handsome Apple iPod arrived with its better battery, vast storage capacity, and chic white earbuds—and private listening exploded.

Today, every mobile phone and tablet is also a fully functioning audio player, almost always equipped with earbuds.

Through all this high fidelity development, the highly evolved human ear has remained extremely sensitive—and vulnerable.[157] "There's been a pretty significant increase over this time period of hearing loss among American adolescents," says physician-investigator Josef

Shargorodsky, formerly of Brigham and Women's Hospital.[158] The prime culprit, say his colleagues there: "loud sound exposure from music listening."[159]

Dr. Shargorodsky's analysis shows that one in five American adolescents has evidence of at least some mild hearing loss.[160] Yet, young adults tend to downplay the consequences of listening to intense sound, according to an Australian study.[161]

The effects of hearing loss are much more serious than not being able to hear the high notes. Besides causing frustration at work and at home, over a lifetime, "deficient hearing has been linked to a greater risk of dementia, poor cognitive function, and falling," says Frank Lin, an otolaryngology researcher from The Johns Hopkins Hospital.[162] Dr. Lin has observed that when hearing loss is untreated in older adults, it can actually hasten brain shrinkage.

Although hearing naturally degrades slowly with age, you can do a lot not to push the process along. In fact, says the NIH, noise-induced hearing loss is "one hundred percent preventable"—but only if you understand how your ears work.

Your outer ear is shaped like a cup to scoop up sounds and channel them directly into your ear canal. Once inside your head, the sounds enter small cavities lined with tiny sensors called "hair cells."[163] In another of your body's astounding feats, the hair cells transform noise vibrations into electrical signals that zip to your brain, where you perceive them as words, music, and other sounds.[164]

Hair cells are shaped like tendrils and blow in sound waves the way blades of grass blow in the breeze. Like strong wind, strong waves of noise cause the hair cells to bend. If the hair cells are consistently exposed to loud noise, they lose their flexibility and you begin to lose your hearing.[165]

Sound is measured in units called decibels (db). A whisper is about 30db and poses no threat to hearing, but factory noise can climb to 85db or more, which is why factory workers often wear earplugs or other forms of hearing protection.[166]

To harmlessly get an idea of the intensity of different noises, try out the National Institute on Deafness and Other Communication Disorder's interactive tool at DurableHuman.com/SoundRuler.

Meanwhile, the volume of the average cellphone can boom up to 105db. That may not seem much noisier than a factory, but because sound intensity increases exponentially, it's actually about one hundred times louder.[167] "If you were to listen at the maximum volume, you really could only listen for about five minutes a day before you'd start to increase your risk for hearing loss," says Brian Fligor, former Diagnostic Audiology director at Boston Children's Hospital.

That's why Apple's iPhone user guide warns:

> *To prevent possible hearing damage, do not listen at high volume levels for long periods.*

In-ear headphones, also called earbuds, plug right into the ear canal. Earbud quality varies, but the set packed with a phone is at the bottom of the heap. Since cheaper earbuds don't convey the full spectrum of musical sound, the user compensates by turning up the volume along with their own potential for hearing damage.

At the airport on the way home after the wedding, we stopped in at an electronics store. After Brian explained he wanted to listen to music but also block office noise, the clerk pointed us to "sound isolating" earphones. Developed for musicians and audio crews working at concerts, the earphones deliver a wide spectrum of "clean" sound so it's possible to listen at a lower volume. We bought Brian a pair as a parting gift.

But as important as it is to protect hearing, you always have to be aware of a product's impact on overall durability. For instance, Brian often rides his bike to work and he needs to hear sirens and other sound cues. For that reason, it's not safe for him to use earbuds when he's riding. They are also outlawed for motor vehicle operators in many U.S. states, according to the American Automobile Association.[168]

If you're on a bike, you also don't want to deprive yourself of one of the main benefits: being refreshed by the sounds of nature.

Durable Human Designs for Maintaining Your Hearing

When it's safe to use earbuds or headphones, follow these NIH instructions:

- First, turn down the volume on your digital device to the lowest level.
- After donning your earbuds or headphones, increase the volume slowly until you can hear the sound clearly, but not loudly.
- If someone standing next to you can also hear what you are listening to, reduce the volume to avoid damaging your ears.

If you will be mowing the lawn or otherwise exposed to loud noise for more than a few minutes, earplugs can help protect your hearing.

Here's how to use the common foam type, according to the NIH Noisy Planet website:

- With clean hands, roll the earplug into a small, thin snake.
- Pulling the top of the ear up and back, slide the rolled-up earplug into the ear.
- For at least twenty seconds, gently hold the earplug in place as it expands to fill the ear canal. Earplugs have a good seal if someone speaking next to you sounds muffled.

Your home can be noisy, too. Sounds are additive, so turning up the TV to hear it over the vacuum significantly boosts the overall noise load.

Some rules of ear for the household:

- Set TVs, radios, video games, and music to the lowest volume at which they can be heard clearly.
- If someone in your household has trouble hearing the TV, turn on closed captioning so they can read the words on the screen. (Conversely, my workaround when watching TV with my dad is to wear my earbuds as an earplug substitute.)
- Curtains, cushions, and upholstered chairs soften loud noises. Cover bare floors with carpet and area rugs.
- Isolate loud noise. For example, close the door to the laundry room while the washer is running.
- Buy quieter appliances. The noise level of a product is often listed on the label or the online information page.
- Keep outside noises out.
  - Fill cracks around windows, doors, and places where pipes and wires enter the house.
  - Close doors and windows to shut out the noise of lawn-mowing and other loud activities.

Kids need their sense of hearing in order to grow and develop normally. "Only through hearing and imitating speech can children adapt their articulation, discover the meanings of words, and ultimately learn how to construct sentences," explains Christine Jones, director of research at Phonak, a Swiss hearing systems firm.

Durable Human Designs for Protecting Kids' Ears

- Encourage babies and very young children to play with toys that don't have batteries or plugs. (Non-electronic play things like balls and blocks also stimulate imagination, creativity, and three-dimensional thinking.[169])

- If you buy an electronic toy, pre-set it to a low volume before giving to a child.
- Teach older kids how to safely set the volume on cellphones and MP3 players. Consider investing in higher quality earbuds and headphones than those supplied with the devices.

If at any time, your child or you are not wearing earplugs and sounds seem muffled, have your hearing checked.

In several European countries, Australia, and the United States, you can take a screening test privately over the phone to help you decide if you need a full-scale hearing evaluation. In the United States, find the test at Durablehuman.com/USNationalHearingTest.

You also need to watch for the visual effects of the digital age.

The Eyes Have (Had) It

Way back in 2009, in the very first Durable Human blog post, I quoted renowned biologist E. O. Wilson. He predicted that video games would be the future of education. "We're going through a rapid transition now," he said. "We're about to leave print and textbooks behind."

Wilson believes games actually teach kids the old-fashioned way: "They went with adults and they learned everything they needed to learn by participating in the process."[170]

Participatory learning is even more achievable today. A teacher and class can explore the rainforest—floor to canopy—without a plane ticket or bug bite. But the screen-based approach is a whole new experience for the human eye.

Eye strain is part of a spectrum of modern-age ailments optometrists call computer vision syndrome (CVS).[171] Also known as digital eye strain, CVS affects almost everyone who uses a computer.

Reading on a screen is different from reading on paper. Computer monitors have an imperceptible flicker that forces your eyes to constantly focus and re-focus on what you read. Switching your focus from the flickering screen to the papers on your desk strains your eyes even more.

Screen reading can cause dry eyes because you blink up to 66 percent less than when you read on paper. If you stare at screens for a long time, you may also develop the bleary-eyed, hard-to-focus, temporary condition known as nearwork-induced transient myopia.[172]

Signs you may be experiencing CVS:

- Red, teary, or irritated eyes
- Blurred vision
- Headache
- Neck and back pain

Thankfully, if you pay attention to your body, your workspace, and how you manage your time, you can minimize—and maybe even eliminate—the effects of CVS.

Durable Human Designs for Avoiding Computer Vision Syndrome

According to the American Optometric Association, the quickest and easiest way to maintain durable vision is to abide by the **20-20-20 rule:**

After 20 minutes using a screen, look away for 20 seconds at something at least 20 feet in the distance.

The 20-20-20 rule will help you even more if you gaze out at something green (see chapter 3).

Adjusting your screen can also help you manage CVS. Some more suggestions from the American Optometric Association:

- Dim overhead lighting to minimize glare.
- Eliminate reflections by angling your screen away from windows or closing shades.
- Position your desk lamp to cast light evenly over your work.
- Especially when you read and write, place the screen slightly below eye level and about 20 inches away, or the length of your outstretched arm with the palm touching the side of your display.
- Position reference books and papers at about the same level as your screen.

The default factory settings on your display may not be the best for your eyes. If you go into the control panel, you can adjust several settings including:

- Brightness
- Contrast
- Text font size
- Color temperature

Color temperature is a measure of the levels of red, green, and blue light emitted by a color display. Blue light has a short wavelength and is most associated with eye strain. (My eyes felt better immediately when I decreased the blue light level on my laptop.)

Durable Human Designs for a Child's Workspace

Just as your child can't fit into your clothes, he or she doesn't fit your workspace. Where kids work:

- The desk or table top should be about elbow height (theirs, not yours).
- Feet should rest comfortably on the floor.
- Like you, a child should look down slightly at a monitor or screen, which should be positioned about the child's arm's length away.

Kids using small screens such as phones should only do quick tasks, such as texting. Articles, reports, and books should be written and read on larger screens.

But, whether you are a child or an adult—there's one more inconvenient truth about using wireless digital devices that affects overall durability.

Know The Glow

Because the human species developed amid sunlight, lightning, and other natural sources of energy, we have evolved into bio-electrical creatures.

Tiny electrical currents flow within us. Without them, we simply wouldn't work—not our hearts, not our muscles, and definitely not our brains.[173]

Electrical impulses jump from cell to cell in your body the same way electricity flows through a wire.[174] When you stub your toe, impulses zoom along nerve cells from your foot to your brain as a tipoff you need to say "ouch." (Your ability to feel pain—known as *nociception*—is another of your amazing human senses.)

Messages crisscrossing the brain generate enough electrical activity to alter blood flow. The change in flow can be measured with something called functional magnetic resonance imaging (fMRI), a technique that has led to many of the discoveries discussed in this book.

Because the brain is so crucial to our existence, our bodies have developed special ways to protect it. The skull, for instance, is essentially a helmet that shields the spongy organ within from bumps and trauma.

A special membrane protects your brain against harmful substances circulating in your bloodstream. This blood-brain barrier is why humans so seldom have brain infections.

But all the while we evolved these powerful brain defenses, digital devices did not exist, so our bodies were not prepared for their arrival.

Enter: The Glow.

A mobile phone is essentially a mini radio transmission tower. As Apple says in the user manual, "iPhone transmits and receives radio frequency (RF) energy through its antennas."[175] The heat of RF energy, at much higher levels, cooks hot dogs in a microwave oven.

I call the energy emanating from an operating wireless device *The Glow*.

The Glow

The Glow from a switched-on cellphone is most intense immediately around the phone, but quickly drops off with distance. At ten inches away, The Glow from a device is one hundred times less intense than when it is pressed against your skull.[176]

That's why wireless manufacturers pack written warnings with all new phones advising you to leave close to an inch of space between you and your operating device. This is the verbiage from Apple:

> *When carrying iPhone, keep it 1.5cm (5/8 inch) or more away from your body to ensure exposure levels remain at or below the maximum levels.*

Because The Glow is electromagnetic in nature, it can interfere with other types of electronics, such as hearing aids and pacemakers. T-Mobile, for instance, cautions pacemaker wearers to always keep their phones at least six inches away from their bodies and never in a breast pocket. If pacemaker wearers hear scratchiness or interference on calls, they are told to "turn your phone OFF immediately."[177]

History of The Glow

No one paid much attention to The Glow until health researchers noted a troubling trend. It appeared that some very rare brain cancers[178] seemed to be occurring more frequently among heavy cellphone users.[179] "Heavy use," in this case, was holding a cellphone to the head for at least thirty minutes a day over a ten-year period.[180]

Dan Brown, for instance, was a football defensive coordinator at California State University in Fresno. He succumbed to a tumor adjacent to his ear canal.

"We didn't know your phone emits radiation," Brown's wife Mindy regretfully recalls. "We joked about it. My husband's ear would get bright red and he'd have to hold his phone out to here during his recruiting calls. He lived on his phone for two decades."[181]

Rich Farther died on his twenty-ninth birthday from the brain cancer, gliosarcoma. "He was a heavy user for ten years," recalls the young man's father. "He specifically relied on a cellphone for his daily use for everything."[182]

The brain isn't the only part of the body not prepared for constant contact with wireless devices.

After Tiffany Frantz received her first cellphone at age fifteen, she would routinely stow it underneath the edge of her bra. By age twenty-one, she had developed breast cancer.

"I am convinced that her cellphone has caused her breast cancer," says Tiffany's mom, Traci. "We never took it seriously until after she was diagnosed. No one ever told us that this was a very bad idea."[183]

In the past, breast cancer among women in their twenties and thirties has been very uncommon, accounting for less than 5 percent of all cases. Of those few, most had a family history of the disease.[184] That's why cancer specialists wrote about Tiffany and three other young women in the journal *Case Reports in Medicine*.[185] None of the four had a family history or a gene mutation that made them particularly prone to breast cancer. All had tumors exactly where they had stowed their phones.

The journal report also features twenty-one-year-old Shea Hartman. Her doctor described calcifications appearing on her mammogram as "exactly the size and shape of the length and width of her cellphone."[186]

Men, too, have developed cancer beneath their shirt pockets.[187]

"A cellphone's sporadic microwave radiation seeps directly into soft fatty tissue of the breast," warns epidemiologist Devra Davis, author of *Disconnect: The Truth About Cell Phone Radiation, What the Industry Has Done to Hide It, and How to Protect Your Family.*

Silicon Valley breast cancer radiologist June Chen concurs: "Until further data either supports it or disproves it, I would keep cellphones away from the body, in particular the breasts."[188]

Traci Frantz wishes the maker of Tiffany's phone had been more obvious about warnings. As she told CBS News, "Had there been a statement on the outside of the box stating what is already stated within the owner's manual about keeping cellphones away from direct contact with the skin, we could have taken precautions to make sure her cellphone was kept in a safe place *off* her body."

At the urging of hundreds of scientists from the United States and at least thirteen other countries, the World Health Organization eventually took a stand on The Glow, concluding that the electromagnetic fields of operating wireless devices are "possibly carcinogenic to humans" and advising:

> *It is important that additional research be conducted into the long-term, heavy use of mobile phones. Pending the availability of such information, it is important to take pragmatic measures to reduce exposure such as hands-free devices or texting.*

The official position of the Federal Communications Commission (FCC) is that "there is no scientific evidence that proves that wireless phone use can lead to cancer or to other health problems, including headaches, dizziness, or memory loss." But the FCC goes on to state:

> *The most effective means to reduce exposure are to hold the*

cell phone away from the head or body and to use a speaker-phone or hands-free accessory.[189]

The National Cancer Institute echoes the FCC:

Reserve the use of cell phones for shorter conversations or for times when a landline phone is not available. Use a hands-free device, which places more distance between the phone and the head of the user.

CNET, a well-known website that reviews consumer digital devices, concurs: "Though each manufacturer varies the wording, all advise that your phone could exceed [the U.S. government's RF energy limit] if you don't hold it at a short distance from your body while it is transmitting." (Recall that a "short distance" is close to an inch.)

The Glow also appears to cause potential problems for would-be fathers.

Fertility researchers in the United States and Australia have discovered that sperm regularly exposed to cellphone energy may become confused and lethargic.

After reviewing existing studies on the topic, the researchers concluded:

Men using mobile phones have decreased sperm concentration, decreased motility (particularly rapid progressive motility), normal morphology, and decreased viability. These abnormalities seem to be directly related to the duration of mobile phone use.[190]

According to Ashok Agarwal, research director of the Cleveland Clinic Center for Reproductive Medicine, "We speculate that keeping the cell phone in a trouser pocket in talk mode may negatively affect spermatozoa and impair male fertility."[191]

Other Wireless Devices and The Glow

These wireless devices also emit The Glow:

- Tablets
- Laptops
- Bluetooth wireless headsets
- Home cordless phones and phone bases
- Cordless baby monitors
- Wi-Fi routers
- Wireless speakers
- Internet-connected iPods
- Wireless printers

Questions have been raised about whether Apple's and other Wi-fi watches emit worrisome levels of The Glow. According to Apple testing, the tissues in the wrist absorb much less radiation than tissues in the head, so no concern about the wrist is warranted. However, Apple also states:

> *When placing Apple Watch near your face, keep at least 10mm [1 centimeter] of separation to ensure exposure levels remain at or below the as-tested levels.*[192]

It would appear, then, to be on the safe side, it's a good idea to take the watch off before bed to avoid inadvertent extended contact with your head while you are sleeping.

With so many types of wireless devices, health concerns are growing about being in the midst of overlapping waves of The Glow. As software developer Ajay Malik pointed out on NetworkWorld.com, "Each person today carries three to five Wi-Fi devices (phone, laptop, watch, tablet, to name a few). And, the last time I looked for a Wi-Fi network at my home, I could see over ten Wi-Fi access points (neighbors!)."[193]

For that reason, Malik and others are asking the FCC to study the situation more carefully. As he writes,

> *With the increase of Wi-Fi/radiation exposure today, the limits established before the "wifization" of society may not be good enough.*

Malik recommends that schools and businesses push for what is essentially the durable human design of Wi-Fi networks. One approach, for instance, would basically dim the overall energy emitted by Wi-Fi devices if too many are emitting too much of The Glow at the same time.[194]

Durable Human Designs for Living with The Glow

Here are some strategies for living safely with The Glow, mainly suggested by Devra Davis and mostly pertaining to cellphones and tablets, sources we contact most directly:

- Texting and video calls naturally separate you from The Glow.
- When making voice calls, create space between your phone and your skull by using earbuds, a wired headset, or your speakerphone function.
- Cordless landline phones also emit The Glow, so use the speakerphone function.
- Use a cellphone or tablet case specifically designed to protect you from The Glow.
- Don't sleep with a wireless device such as a phone under your pillow or close to your head on a nightstand.

- Charge your phone away from your sleeping area (which also contributes to a more restful sleep, as we saw in chapter 6).
- Using an alarm clock and a standard watch can reduce your constant need for a phone and reduce your overall exposure to The Glow.
- Look out for few signal bars. They mean your phone is working hard to get a signal, so it is emitting more energy.[195]
- When using a wireless-enabled tablet or laptop, use the device on a hard surface away from your body or on a commercially made protective shield.
- At home and at work, turn off wireless devices you aren't using.

If You Are Pregnant

- Use tablets or laptops away from your body on a hard surface.
- Operate wireless devices at least eight inches away from the abdomen.[196]

When Wearing Pants with Pockets

- Carry your phone on a belt clip.
- If you must pocket your phone, always switch the device off or into airplane mode.
- Use a protective case.

The British firm WaveWall claims its cases, when used correctly, reduce the effects of The Glow by more than 85 percent. Project Manager Harry Gardiner developed the products out of concern for a male friend's infertility problems.[197]

I have a quick workaround for taking a phone call when earbuds or a case aren't handy. You can create about an inch of space between your phone and your ear if you cradle the bottom of the phone in your palm and hook your fingers over the top from behind the phone. Then, rest your fingers—not your phone—against your temple.

Kids and The Glow

Children are even more vulnerable to the effects of The Glow.

As the American Academy of Pediatrics wrote to the FCC:

> *The differences in bone density and the amount of fluid in a child's brain compared to an adult's brain could allow children to absorb greater quantities of RF energy deeper into their brains than adults. It is essential that any new standards for cell phones or other wireless devices be based on protecting the youngest and most vulnerable populations to ensure they are safeguarded through their lifetimes.*[198]

The American Cancer Society also states:

> *Individuals who are concerned about radiofrequency exposure can limit their exposure, including using an ear piece and limiting cell phone use, particularly among children.*[199]

Countries including France, Russia, the U.K. and Zambia either ban cellphone sales intended for child use or actively discourage children from using mobile phones.[200]

Durable Human Designs for Protecting Kids from The Glow

To be on the safe side with babies and toddlers, never place a wireless device in a crib or car seat. It's too easy for a child to touch the device or fall asleep on top of it.

Keep in mind that even airplane mode does not completely eliminate The Glow.

Once you decide your children are mature enough to handle a wireless device, they need to learn the same durable habits that you have:

- Use the speakerphone or earbuds when making calls.
- Never carry an unshielded device in a shirt or pants pocket or tuck it under a bra.
- Unless phones, laptops, and tablets have Wi-Fi turned off, are in airplane mode, or are in protective cases, devices should not be held directly in the lap.

It bears repeating from chapter 6 that your child's bedroom is a sanctuary and should be free of things that go beep in the night. Toward that end, encourage your child to:

- Charge devices out of the bedroom in a place such as the kitchen, hallway, or your bathroom.
- Wear a watch and use an alarm clock to wake up instead of a phone.

Managing kids' use of cellphones in school can be tricky. When a middle school in New Zealand tried to ban phones in the classroom, boys started texting from inside their front pants pockets, thus exposing their delicate sex organs to The Glow for up to ten hours a day.[201]

Some researchers recommend that, rather than banning phones, schools could instead require students to keep their phones in plain sight on top of their desks. That way kids develop the discipline to work independently alongside, but not always directly including, their phones.

Myopia Rising

One final thought about the interplay between our bodies, nature, and technology.

Researchers in Taiwan were puzzled about a difference between the same-aged kids at two different schools. All were seven- to eleven-year olds, but at one of the schools the kids were more likely to need glasses. They had myopia, the technical term for being near-sighted. They could see objects clearly up close, but things in the distance looked blurry. (Some of the kids in the myopic group would have needed glasses anyway but, statistically, not all of them.)

Assuming children in both schools used screens for about the same amount of time, why did their vision differ? It turned out that the group needing glasses hardly ever went out for recess.

Thus, the researchers concluded:

> *Increasing time spent outdoors may be a simple strategy by which to reduce the risk of developing myopia and its progression in children and adolescents.*

Data from the study show that the chance a child will develop myopia is reduced by two percent for every hour spent outdoors per week.[202]

This is but one more example of how science is proving we can steer ourselves in a durable direction, for everything from our eyesight to our emotions.

CHAPTER 8:

MANAGE YOUR MIND

The real problem is not whether machines think, but whether men do.

B.F. Skinner, behavioral psychologist

Throughout this book, we've seen how functional MRI is pulling back the curtain on your cerebral organ-in-chief. Perhaps the most amazing revelation is that your brain is plastic. No, not plastic like little green army men, but plastic, as in flexible.

Contrary to previous assumptions that neural pathways in our brains are set by the time we reach adulthood, fMRI has revealed they change throughout life, depending on what we think and do.

"Our brains are constantly being shaped all the time, wittingly and unwittingly, most of the time, just being pushed around like a sailboat which has lost its rudder," observes Richard Davidson of the University of Wisconsin-Madison. But there is hope, as Davidson underscored at the 2015 Mindful Leadership Summit:

> *We can take more responsibility for shaping our minds and brains.*[203]

That means you don't always have to be a victim of external forces. It may be possible for you to reattach your mind's rudder.

This revelation comes exactly when we are grappling with a new predator of our time and autonomy: the firehose of constant input.

It was early in 2011 that I realized I was maxed out. Grousing to my daughter about the many thousands of emails piled in my multiple inboxes, it struck me:

> *I could read all day and all night, ad infinitum, and never finish.*

Sure, I may eventually catch up on those particular emails, but more would pile up as I dealt with them and I would never have time to follow up on every attachment, link, and post.

My life is in stark contrast to my father's. I remember the day—he was 87 at the time—my dad announced he was happy. "I get up. I take care of your mother and myself. Then I can do whatever I want for the rest of the day"—which was basically reading in his favorite chair with jazz on the radio.

What my father does not do is constantly look at his phone. He checks email every few *days*.

As I watched him, I wondered: can I ever be truly contented—happy to *just sit there*, without a care in the world? Sadly, I'm afraid not. Barring a horrible worldwide disaster, the firehose of email and posts and who-knows-what future time-consuming founts of information will never shut off.

To remain hopeful in our predicament is to learn how to manage the firehose.

That Frazzled Feeling

Have you ever noticed, when you've been working hard a while—maybe scanning job listings or rushing to meet a deadline—you need to read the lines over and over to get them to stick? It's like when you've gorged on a big dinner, but it's your mind that has the *too full* feeling.

That's when you need a brain break.

"The solution is not to stop using the tools that are so valuable at providing connection and knowledge. The trick is to learn when to use them and when to put them aside," concludes California State University psychologist Larry Rosen.[204]

How often does your mind need a break? Considering the amount of email, information, and stimulation you face every day, Rosen says *every one to two hours*. To continue beating your aching head against the virtual wall becomes a losing battle. To be productive in the long run, you need to take a break.

Let that sink in for just a moment.

The longer you push at a task after you notice that frazzled feeling, the more time it will take to get the job done. So, by giving your mind a few moments to decompress, *you can do more in less time*. Isn't that what we're all after, anyway?

Another advantage of brain breaks: they inject some unscheduled wild time into your day.

In his book, *iDisorder: Understanding Our Obsession with Technology and Overcoming Its Hold on Us*, Rosen says a great relief for your brain is to step outside:

> *Taking a nature break for just a few minutes can decrease stress and increase our brain's ability to process information.*

Durable Human Designs for Decompressing

Here are more of Rosen's suggestions for brief brain breaks:

- Have a light conversation (not an argument).
- Laugh, perhaps by reading or remembering something funny.
- Listen to music.
- Look at something you consider beautiful, such as artwork.

If you have (or need) more time:

- Take a bath or shower.
- Practice a foreign language.
- Play a musical instrument.
- Do Sudoku or a crossword.
- Exercise.

Many adults have rediscovered the mental sanctuary of coloring books. Another type of relaxation, known as an autonomous sensory meridian response (ASMR),[205] can occur when people watch recordings of monotonous everyday sounds and actions. The website SootheTube.com makes a science of curating ASMR videos.

While writing this book, I got in the habit of doing one minute of jumping jacks every hour I worked at my keyboard. I was delighted to discover that when I returned—more often than not—a fresh idea or turn of phrase had popped into my head.

"What's happening there is that quick bouts of movement cause quick hits of hyperoxygenation [enrichment with more oxygen] within the brain," explains Florida State University sports physiologist John Groppel. The result? You have more energy, more focus, and hopefully you'll generate new ideas.[206]

Even if you're stuck at your desk or in a meeting, you can still take a subtle brain break by doing something else on Rosen's list: purposeful breathing.

Andrew Weil is a physician of integrative medicine, a specialty combining traditional Western medical treatment with alternative techniques. According to Dr. Weil, to breathe purposefully is to take slower, deeper, and more conscious breaths. "By doing so, you are making your body function better, you're quieting your mind, and normalizing your nervous system."[207]

By paying attention to your breath, you can also lasso runaway thoughts. That's a Jewel 1 skill, better known as being *mindful*—something I had to learn the hard way.

My Painful Meeting with Mindfulness

It was a Saturday morning at the end of winter. I was about to tackle a long list of home projects when I took a quick squint at my email. A "state of the state" presentation was happening at the local town hall and I had a sudden urge to be there.

Thinking the sun had melted the remaining snow on the trail, I thought I'd get some exercise if I rode my bicycle, which happens to be the folding, space-saving type. After a quick assembly, the handlebars didn't look quite right, but they felt secure so I was off and rolling.

After I'd been in the meeting a while, I grew anxious to get to my chores, so I slipped out and was soon rushing back toward home. Up ahead on the trail, I saw two people walking and a small patch of ice. But as I tried to pass between them, my handlebars buckled and I crashed to the pavement.

Stunned and embarrassed, I was helped to my feet by one of the walkers while the other secured my handlebars—*carefully* this time. After offering a shaky thanks, I winced my way home—lucky to get away with only a cracked rib and a bruised ego.

It wasn't until later I realized *why* the accident happened.

The revelation came at an unlikely conference held near the cradle of digital development—California's Silicon Valley. Although the Wisdom 2.0 conference is packed with entrepreneurs and executives from the likes of Twitter, Facebook, and LinkedIn, they aren't there to talk technology. The gathering is meant to connect people "in ways that are beneficial to our own well-being, effective in our work, and useful to the world."

I was there to learn what "ways" they were talking about.

Wisdom 2.0's founder, Soren Gordhamer, is a former tech professional who was nearly devoured by the digital world. "What most mattered to me was knowing if I had received any messages in the two minutes since I last checked," he recalls in his book *Wisdom 2.0, The New Movement Toward Purposeful Engagement in Business and in Life.*[208]

Intellectually, Gordhamer knew how to achieve life balance, but he was living otherwise. Too busy to taste his food or get enough sleep, his time with family and friends had dwindled to almost nothing: "By feeling one thing internally while my actions expressed completely different priorities, my life was out of alignment."

Sensing he was about to self-destruct, he decided to "bring consciousness" into his actions. He would start to be *mindful.*

Arianna Huffington became mindful when she woke up in a pool of her own blood.

After two frantic years setting up *The Huffington Post*, she fainted in her office, breaking her cheekbone on her desk as she fell to the floor.

That's how many people become mindful—painfully. "Our entry points in this journey are often points of breakdown," she confided to a rapt Wisdom 2.0 audience.[209]

It was then I realized why I crashed: I wasn't being mindful. As my hands had latched the parts of my bike together, my mind was racing miles ahead. I was disjointed, just like those Gordhamer describes in his book:

> *Walk down the street of any major city and most people are essentially "somewhere else," either because they are on their phone or are daydreaming about some future moment or reliving a past one. This moment, the one we are living now, is so often missed.*

Harvard researchers tracked thousands of people through a specially made app, proving Gordhamer's point: Almost half the time during a typical day, participants' minds were not focused on what they were doing.[210]

My daughter Shannon teaches yoga, an ancient practice seen as a physical manifestation of mindfulness. I love her interpretation:

> *Mindfulness is accepting your state in the moment—living in it—not trying to escape through technology or distraction. It's about allowing the mind noise to settle.*

My mind was mighty noisy when I crashed on my bike.

These days, rather than jamming as much as possible into every spare moment, I try to see in-between times as a chance to mentally switch gears. I ask myself Gordhamer's question:

> *How do I skillfully finish what I am doing so I can enter the next event with clarity and focus?*

Durable Human Designs for Being More Mindful

Two methods for becoming more mindful are easy to remember and can be done subtly in many situations.

The first is the STOP technique, introduced by psychologist Elisha Goldstein in his book, *The NOW Effect: How This Moment Can Change the Rest of Your Life.*[211]

STOP stands for:

S: Stop what you're doing.

T: Take a slow, purposeful breath.

O: Observe what's happening around you, acknowledging how you feel inside. If you are thinking of something in the future or the past, bring your thoughts back to the present moment.

P: Proceed, but only after asking yourself: *What's most important for me to pay attention to right now?*

The second exercise can pull your mind and body back together when you're jittery, such as waiting for a job interview. On the website MindBodyGreen.com, meditation teacher Charlene Richard shared "5-4-3-2-1":

- Look around and mentally take note of *five* things you *see.*
- Now, mentally note *four* things you *feel,* such as the chair you're sitting on or the breeze from a ceiling fan.
- Next, bring your attention to your ears and *three* things you *hear.*
- Then, name *two* things you smell or can *imagine smelling.*
- Finally, notice *one* thing you can taste or you would *like* to taste.

"You may need to do it more than once," Richard advises. "But by bringing your attention to the present moment—using your senses— you stop your mind from focusing on the worst-case scenario."

When it comes to kids, those who practice mindfulness in school are more attentive and can better control their emotions. That's according to Inner Explorer, a school-based mindful awareness program. Inner Explorer participants also tend to do better in science, math, and reading—and their teachers report feeling less stressed.[212] In Flint, Michigan, the school system is using Inner Explorer in an effort to counteract the damage that may have been done to the brains of kids who drank lead-tainted water.

One of Rosen's mind-resetting techniques that can become a life-long pursuit is the practice of meditation. *TIME* magazine describes meditation as "doing nothing and being tuned into your own mind."[213]

Thousands of years after Buddhist monks began sitting quietly and focusing their thoughts, fMRI now shows meditation induces a specific brainwave pattern. "This wave type has been used as a universal sign of relaxation," observes Øyvind Ellingsen of Norwegian University of Science and Technology.[214]

This is how my daughter describes the benefits of meditation:

You can release the things that are not serving you or applicable to you. It makes decision-making more simple and clear.

According to Harvard psychologist Ron Siegel, if mindfulness is combined with meditation, it "can help us get out of our own way."[215]

Wall Street executive Golbie Kamarei had meditated in her personal life for years before she started a mindful meditation program where she works—BlackRock, the world's largest asset manager. Now, more than 1,300 employees in fifteen countries are in the program. Nine out of ten participants report less stress overall, say their work relationships are smoother, they can better manage their emotions, and feel more compassion for others.[216]

Firms including Twinings tea seller and Virgin Atlantic airline have embraced services such as Headspace.com, which offer mindfulness exercises in bite-sized, online sessions.

Jon Kabat-Zinn was studying molecular biology at MIT when he was introduced to meditation. After years of study and practice, he developed the technique known as Mindfulness-Based Stress Reduction (MBSR). MBSR has since been proven not only to relieve tension, but to lessen a slew of physical problems ranging from pain to high blood pressure to headache. fMRI also shows that MBSR actually shifts activation patterns within the brain toward greater emotional balance and away from fear-based reactions.

Even without full-scale MBSR, simply conjuring up thoughts of nature can have a positive effect on overall health. Patients in a Swedish intensive care unit needed less pain medicine when they gazed at pictures of trees and water.[217]

But, despite revelations about how we can direct ourselves toward calm, most of us are still stuck in mental overdrive.

The Myth of Multi-tasking

Another reason Soren Gordhamer suggests fully completing one task before moving on to the next is to avoid "draining our energy by continuously multi-tasking."

The term *multi-tasking* is actually a misnomer. In fact, for us humans, it isn't really possible.

Though we may *think* we can focus on more than one mental task at the same time, our brains are actually switching very quickly between them. "People can really work in only one frame of reference at a time," says Steven Hoober, author of the book *Designing Mobile Interfaces.*[218]

For instance, when I'm at a conference composing a tweet, in the moments I'm typing the words, I miss what the speaker is saying.

To assess the human ability to multi-task, researchers studied Stanford University students, considered among the brightest in the United States. "Multi-taskers were just lousy at everything," wrote Stanford professor Clifford Nass, a chief investigator.[219] In fact, the more tasks a student tried to do simultaneously, the worse he or she did on subsequent simple tests, such as distinguishing colors and differentiating odd from even numbers.[220]

Other research shows that students who text or check social media in class don't do as well on exams as students who pay attention.[221]

Yet, research by the parenting advice group Common Sense Media shows that three out of four teenagers report they watch TV, interact on social media, or listen to music while doing their homework.[222]

Larry Rosen combats this problem by training his students to spend about a half hour listening in class without checking their phones or social media, then rewarding them with a minute of checking. (I try to do the same thing with myself.)

Your Memory Bucket

To be durable in the digital world is to know how your mind operates. For instance, your working memory is kind of like a bucket. What your mental bucket can carry is known as your cognitive load. Familiar, easy tasks take up less space in the bucket and unfamiliar, complex tasks take up more space and create a greater cognitive load.[223]

Just as your skeleton carries a specific weight range, your mental bucket has a maximum carrying capacity, otherwise known as your cognitive limit. Your limit varies and is affected by what happens to the rest of your body. "Stress, time pressure, and lack of sleep are but a few factors which can decrease the available cognitive resource pool," says East Carolina University technology communications professor Michael Albers.[224]

Deep sea divers, for instance, must constantly monitor their own activities underwater. For novice divers, it may be taxing enough to simultaneously breathe from a tank, swim, and watch for sharks. Adding one more function, such as operating a camera, may be too much to safely manage.

For the same reason, airplane pilots have a "sterile cockpit rule" that forbids idle chatter at times they must concentrate on the critical functions of flying an airplane.[225]

You also need to be aware of your own cognitive resources, especially when you're behind the wheel.

Let's say you're driving in a heavy thunderstorm late at night. Rain pounds the windshield as you strain to read road signs and listen for radio alerts. At that point, if you do one more task—such as answer the phone—you could exceed your cognitive limit. Or, as Steven Hoober points out, "adding another task is a bad thing, no matter how small the task."[226]

Once you pass your cognitive tipping point, your brain—in an effort to free up memory—automatically drops tasks, in no particular order of importance. "Your leaky bucket is happy to discard safety-critical items in favor of trivial ones," as Hoober says.[227] Without even realizing it, you might stop doing something important or focus on something relatively trivial. "This is what happens in lots of accidents," Hoober told me. "People get hung up on—say—their phone call, then drive into another car."

The way our brains jettison functions is "an out of date tactic, from an era of wandering the plains with sticks when there weren't really high and low priority tasks," concludes Hoober.

Durable Human Designs for Avoiding Cognitive Overload

Because you likely won't realize when you've passed your cognitive tipping point, you need to know if you're getting close. When you show signs of stress—you start to sweat or your heart is racing—is likely the time to stop matters from becoming more complicated.

Often, you can control the overall situation if you minimize one aspect. "So tell the kids to shut up, or move to where you aren't being rained on, or turn off the radio—and then you can concentrate," Hoober advises.

These strategies can help to keep your composure in pressurized situations:

- Turn off extraneous noises and devices.
- Ask the people around you to minimize conversation.
- Try to delegate a task to someone else—such as monitoring your phone—so you can focus your reasoning and ingenuity on the problem at hand.

Being aware of your cognitive limit is a Jewel 1 skill that not only makes you more self-reliant, it could save your life.

Another type of digital-age overload may not be life-threatening, but still heaps stress on your average day.

Managing the Firehose

As current curator of the TED thought leadership conferences, Chris Anderson gets a torrent of email. He pines for the good old days when people couldn't virtually "barge into someone's house or office and expect, then and there, twenty minutes of your thoughtful, focused attention. If you're not careful, it can gobble up most of your week."[228]

Gobbling has become so easy.

Let's say I get an email about a new grant opportunity. The description of the application process goes on and on and soon I'm tired of reading. What can I do then? Forward the email to a colleague with the comment, "Should we bring this up at our next meeting?"

Presto! I dumped my thinking time onto someone else I hope will read the whole thing and get back to me. In one sentence, I have become an Evil Time Dictator.

Anderson calls that maneuver a "tragedy of the commons." The commons, in this case, is the worldwide pool of attention. "Instant communication makes it a little too easy to grab a piece of that attention," says Anderson. "The result of all those little acts of grabbing is a giant drain on our time, energy, and sanity."

Anderson won the Triple Crown (skill-building, enhancing relationships, and carving out time for curiosity) when he composed the Email Charter—ten simple rules to stop us from being so lazy and inconsiderate.

Durable Human Designs for Better Email Etiquette

Five of Anderson's rules are especially useful:

- Respect your recipient's time. If you start the email process, you control the time you cost others. Be honest with yourself before you press *Send*. If you know you're dumping your thinking time on someone else, don't do it.

- Short or slow does not equal rude. Everyone else is also drowning in information. Keep that in mind if someone takes a while to get back to you. If their reply is brief, be grateful, not miffed.

- Avoid open-ended questions. Try not to send an email ending with a question like "Thoughts?" Better to give the recipient finite choices, such as: "Would you like me to (a) call, (b) stop by, or (c) butt out?"

- Avoid low-value, high-cost replies. Not every email needs a response. If you get an email saying, "Thanks for your note. I'm in!", think first whether a reply is truly necessary. Tossing off the single word "Great!" will cost someone time.

- Use EOM and NNR. If you can, reduce your message to one phrase and put it in the subject line along with the letters EOM—End of Message—indicating there's no content in the body of the email. If you do need to write a message, but it doesn't require an answer, end your content with the letters NNR—No Need to Respond.

Advertisements are another source of information overload. I avoid many ads by using the search engine DuckDuckGo, which bypasses the companies that feed off data collected in Google searches.

Not only does DuckDuckGo not track you, its "!bang" feature cuts through landing pages and takes you directly where you want to go. If you want information about ants, for instance, by typing "!W ants" in the DuckDuckGo search box, you go right to the "Ants" page on Wikipedia. (DuckDuckGo uses "!bang" shorthand, such as "W" for Wikipedia.)

Just knowing DuckDuckGo exists gives me hope that, as more products come out that threaten to gobble up our time and autonomy, enlightened professional designers will come to the rescue with ways to fight back.

Finally, another helpful Alt-Brain is subtly but surely redirecting our own.

The GPS Effect

A Facebook post by an award-winning industrial design student is telling. Having just graduated from college, a number of companies were vying for his prodigious skills, but he almost missed his first interview, as he later related:

> *Having a GPS has completely destroyed my ability to know where I am, or where I am going.*

Maybe this has happened to you: you're driving where you've driven many times before, but your navigation system tells you to go another way, so you do and end up going the wrong way, *despite your better judgment.*

"It's the voice—we as human beings are voice-obsessed," said Stanford professor Nass in his book *The Man Who Lied to His Laptop: What Machines Teach Us About Human Relationships.*

Even at one-day old, babies can distinguish human voices from other sounds, according to Nass: "The fact that the GPS has a voice makes it more powerful than any other technology without a voice."[229]

Thankfully, though, we don't always depend on digital navigation. We continue to use the maps in our heads to get around our homes, offices, and on familiar streets.

We should keep it up, too, because the hippocampus shrinks from lack of use, a fact which worries McGill University neuroscientist Veronique Bohbot. Based on her research, Bohbot believes, because society is becoming so dependent on digital wayfinding, dementia is likely going to happen earlier to more people than ever before.[230]

Durable Human Designs for Self-Navigation

To maintain the navigational parts of your brain, Bohbot's message is clear: use it or lose it.[231]

These are her suggestions for keeping your hippocampus in gear:[232]

- Use a hybrid approach when driving: follow the GPS to your destination, but try to rely on your memory to get back.
- Before heading out, review the directions and get an overview of where you're going.
- When you walk, whether using a GPS or not, notice significant buildings, natural features, and street signs along the way. Those landmarks will help you form a mental map so it will be easier to get around from memory.
- In familiar areas when not using GPS, try new routes and shortcuts.
- If giving directions to someone else, sketch out a map from a bird's eye view.

Most of Bohbot's tips for overall brain health look durably familiar:

- Get enough sleep.
- Exercise 30 minutes a day, five days a week.
- Eat a diet rich in vegetables, nuts, legumes, and Omega-3 oil.
- Don't eat animal products more than four times a week.
- Practice meditation and deep breathing.

Since there's always a chance your phone battery will die or you'll lose the satellite signal, it may sound quaint, but having a paper map is a good backup. They're still available online from Rand McNally and for purchase in the U.S. at AAA stores.

Now that you're aware of many ways you can direct your Self toward durability, what happens next is up to you.

CHAPTER 9:
EMBRACE YOUR NATURE

Be ashamed to die until you have won some victory for humanity.

Horace Mann, politician and education reformer

My dog and I were heading home from a walk when a woman approached us on the path. She wore shorts and carried hand weights. Her dark, shoulder-length braids were flecked with grey. She smiled as she passed and gave the dog a quick word of greeting.

I had never seen the woman before, but I knew exactly how she got there.

Years earlier—when my youngest child, Reilly, was a little boy—we moved to a new neighborhood. After we'd lived there a while, I wanted to walk with him to a nearby botanical garden park. Almost as soon as we set off, though, our neighborhood's short segment of sidewalk abruptly ended.

As we trudged through the grass along the roadside, we came upon the fresh detritus of a car accident. A rear view mirror glinted in the sun and tape from a crushed cassette lay beneath lengths of clear plastic medical tubing.

Years later, I would meet the father of the college student who was airlifted to the hospital from that place the night before. Her car had been struck head-on by a truck rounding the curve. Her life was never the same.

My son and I made it safely to the park and back, but afterward I couldn't help ponder the fragility of life and what could have happened to us that day.

A few weeks later, our newly-elected county supervisor wanted to meet with constituents and learn about their needs. Though I'd never spoken with a public official before, I decided to tell her about our lack of sidewalks. A neighbor helped me pull together data about the growth of our local population and in the number of cars on the streets.

"Very interesting," the supervisor told me. "If you can find other people who also care about this, come back and see me."

As I thought about how to reach out to friends and neighbors, I studied a map of the area. I was surprised to see, all around where we lived, there were green patches signifying parks. Yet, getting to any of them by foot or bike was nearly impossible.

That's it! I thought. If we had a network of paths, our community could easily walk or ride a bicycle to the parks, other neighborhoods, and even a nearby town.

Next, I introduced myself to the manager of the botanical garden who generously allowed his indoor facility to be used for a meeting. And so it was, on a cold November evening, members of my community said *yes*—they *did* want to visit our parks without always having to drive. Some people even volunteered to help make it happen.

The rest, as they say, is history. Our supervisor gave her backing, our homeowners association sent me to a conference about how to plan active communities, and county residents eventually voted to fund construction of the trail network (which, by the time it was built ten years later, connected us to a newly redeveloped town center).

Today—after thousands of hours of meetings, letter writing, and agreements struck in the nick of time—new sidewalks and trails weave through our locale, and the woman who passed me and my dog can walk where she wants to go.

The point of this story is that your ideas can change the world, too–as long as you act on them.

Begin NOW

When my son Brian moved away from home, he left behind a shiny silver book, *The War of Art: Break Through the Blocks and Win Your Inner Creative Battle.*

The author, Steven Pressfield, writes, "It is our obligation to enact our own internal revolution, a private insurrection in our own skulls." The revolution erupts from our Selves, he continues, "the epicenter of our being: our genius, our soul, the unique and priceless gift we were put on earth to give and that no one else has but us."

Start with your Self.

When you wake up in the morning, take a few minutes to think before you pick up your phone. Arrange your home and workspace to capitalize on your personal assets. Cast off habits that get in your way.

It may take only a tweak or pinch.

Cover the light on the thermostat and you'll sleep more soundly. If your son charges his phone in your bathroom tonight, he may know more on the test tomorrow. If you wear a watch instead of holding your phone, your hands will be free to give him a back rub.

Amplify your durability.

Place snacks on a shelf out of sight and your kids will learn patience and the meaning of *treat.* Slide your tablet in a drawer and your toddler will naturally gravitate toward blocks or an imaginary friend. Pop gadgets in a basket and you might catch the telling shadow crossing your daughter's face.

My dentist replaced the panels over her exam room ceiling lights with translucent plastic inserts of puffy clouds and blue sky. In Springhill Suites hotels, motifs of green leaves and blue waves decorate carpet and wallpaper. Remember that nature makes you feel good.

In your own way, for your own family, and in your own place, build physical activity irresistibly into people's lives.

Tell your friends: unless kids climb, explore, and have a sense of direction, they won't be durable adults. Remind them kids need wild time to brew the ideas that will keep our species afloat.

Before any decision, ask yourself: will this lead to durability? If technology is part of the solution, will it support human ingenuity, creativity, and heart?

Seize the power of the Triple Crown to advance your:

 SELF-RELIANCE

 GENUINE RELATIONSHIPS

 CURIOSITY

Every day: do things your smartphone can't.

Watch the sun set. Sniff dewy magnolias. Walk barefoot in the grass. Get lost in a book. Make something. Giggle with your baby. Hug your teenager. Daydream. Sing and dance. Play charades. Tell stories. Linger with someone older and wiser. Take a nap. Listen to crickets. Follow your heart.

Savor the privilege of being human.

THANK YOU

Now that you know my durable human ideas, I'd love to hear yours. Please write to me at jj@durablehuman.com or over at the Durable Human Facebook community. Please also share your thoughts about the book with other readers.

Because you have generously shared your precious time with me, I made you a gift: a handy checklist of the durable human designs in this book. Find it at DurableHuman.com/Gift.

So, until we speak again, I wish you the very best in your durable pursuits.

Yours in curiosity,

Jenifer Joy Madden

ACKNOWLEDGMENTS

And forget not that the earth delights to feel your bare feet and the winds long to play with your hair.

Kahlil Gibran, from his poem "Clothes Chapter X"

I am grateful to all the generous people who helped create this book, and to you for reading it.

I am particularly beholden to my ace editorial team: Michele Matrisciani, for brilliantly sculpting the Durable message; Rebecca Gholson, for nailing down the details; and Lucy Beck, M.D., muse of all things medical.

My gratitude also goes to designer Patty Wallace for always leading me in a beautiful direction and managing to squeeze in one more phone call after the kids were in bed. Thanks, too, to illustrator Marisa Fritz for unfailingly drawing on her talents as she was driven across the country.

I appreciate all the smart, patient people who answered my questions and whose designs, demonstrations, and ideas form the foundation of this book, especially Mark Fenton, Soren Gordhamer, Tristan Harris, Steven Hoober, Marghanita Hughes. Arianna Huffington, Richard J. Jackson, Elaine Lockard, Richard Louv, Day Martin, Mirta Nieves, Peter Norton, Martin Ogle, Greg Raisman, Michael Rich, Larry Rosen, Jeff Speck, Fr. Jud Weiksnar, and Robert Zarr.

They say you should write what you know, but in my case, I write *whom* I know, so thanks go to my cousins, Jeni Davis and Amy Rubacky, who didn't mind serving as examples. I will be forever grateful for the wise counsel of my friend and writing buddy, Caron Martinez, all the way back to the Last Generation, B.C. I'm thankful, too, for my steadfast partners in the promotion of durable living, Fionnuala Quinn, Jeff Anderson, Catherine Hudgins, Keith Tomlinson, Merrily Pierce, and the Coral Ridge Homeowners Association.

Finally, to my husband, Mark: thank you for your unceasing good humor, encouragement, and love. To my three wonderful children, Shannon, Brian, and Reilly: this book (and my heart) would be nowhere without you. And I'm glad for our dog, Busser, who always wanted to go for a walk.

NOTES

1. Balkam, Stephen. Remarks. Family Online Safety Institute Annual Conference, Washington, D.C., November 10, 2010.

2. "The Last Word: This Is Your Brain on GPS." November 5, 2009. The Week. com.

3. The Diane Rehm Show. 2015. Interview with James Steyer. November 5, 2015.

4. Harris, Tristan. Remarks. Wisdom 2.0 conference, San Francisco, California, March 1, 2015.

5. Infinite Stupidity: A Talk with Mark Pagel. Edge.org. December 15, 2011.

6. Leopold, Aldo. 1949. *A Sand County Almanac, and Sketches Here and There.* New York: Oxford University Press.

7. Grey, C.G.P. 2014. "Humans Need Not Apply," Youtube video. Posted by C.G.P. Grey, August 13, 2014.

8. Sainato, Michael. 2015. "Stephen Hawking, Elon Musk, and Bill Gates Warn About Artificial Intelligence." The Observer.com, August 19, 2015.

9. Wilson, Edward O. Resurgence, Volume 10. 1979.

10. Grey, C.G.P. 2014. "Humans Need Not Apply." Youtube video. Posted by C.G.P. Grey. August 13, 2014.

11. Benazir, Ali. 2011. "What Are the Chances of Your Coming Into Being?" Blog. June 15, 2011.

12. Science Friday. "Scientists Test What the Nose Knows." Audio recording. March 21, 2014.

13. Science Friday. "Is Deep Sea Exploration Worth It?" Radio show. September 18, 2015.

14. Ryan, Liz. 2013. "Putting HUMAN back in Human Resources." Linkedin article. September 24, 2013.

15. Alboher, Marci. 2008. "Sharpening the Soft Skills (Which Aren't Really Touchy-Feely)." New York Times, April 7, 2008.

16. Colvin, Geoff. 2015. "Humans Are Underrated." Fortune, August 1, 2015.

17. Archer, Bruce. 1973. *The Need for Design Education*. London: Royal College of Art.

18. Cornog, Megan, and Dan Gelinne. 2010. Federal Highway Administration. Research and Technology. "World class streets." Public Road, 73(6).

19. Miller, Stephen. 2012. "Brooklyn CB 2 Committee Unanimously Supports Permanent Fowler Plaza." StreetsblogNYC.org.

20. Spool, Jared. 2015. Remarks. MoDevUX, Arlington, Virginia, March 24, 2015.

21. Irwin, Neil. 2013. "These 12 Technologies Will Drive Our Economic Future." Washington Post, May 24, 2013.

22. Wasik, Bill. "In The Programmable World, All Our Objects Will Act As One." Wired, June 2013: 144.

23. Matthews, Dylan. 2015. "I Got A Computer Chip Implanted Into My Hand." Vox.com.

24. Rolston, Mark. Remarks. MoDevUX 2012. Youtube video. Posted by Peter Erickson, May 21, 2012. Washington, D.C., April 2012.

25. Chochinov, Allan. Lecture. Rochester Institute of Technology, February 9, 2011. Rochester, New York.

26. Confino, Jo. 2013. Google Seeks Out Wisdom of Zen Master Thich Nhat Hanh. The Guardian. September 5, 2013.

27. Jerry the Bear. Jerrythebear.com.

28. Colvin, Geoff. 2015. "Humans Are Underrated." Fortune, August 1, 2015.

29. Mehlin, Ellen. "Soft Skills: What Employers Want (And Don't Want) in an Employee." Metropolitan New York Library Council. Metro.org.

30. Robinson, Ken. 2011. *Out of Our Minds: Learning To Be Creative*. West Sussex: Capstone Publishing Ltd.

31. ABC News. 2011. "Man Dies From Blood Clot After Marathon Gaming," reported by Kim Carollo. ABCnews.go.com. August 2, 2011.

32. Netflights blog. "Deep Vein Thrombosis and Flying." Netflights.com.

33. Vlahosapril, James. 2011. "Is Sitting a Lethal Activity?" New York Times Sunday Magazine, April 17, 2011.

34. World Health Organization. 2015. "Diabetes." WHO.int.

35. American Diabetes Association. 2002. Type 2 Diabetes in Children and Young Adults: A 'New Epidemic.' Clinical Diabetes 20(4): 217-218.

36. Vlahosapril, James. 2011. "Is Sitting a Lethal Activity?" New York Times Sunday Magazine, April 17, 2011.

37. Levine, James. 2014. "Killer Chairs: How Desk Jobs Ruin Your Health." Scientific American, November 1, 2014.

38. Recent updates to Oxford Dictionaries. August 2015.

39. Patel, Alpa V., et al. 2010. Leisure Time Spent Sitting in Relation to Total Mortality in a Prospective Cohort of US Adults. American Journal of Epidemiology 172 (4):419-429.

40. Lipska, Kasia. 2014. "The Global Diabetes Epidemic." New York Times, April 25, 2014.

41. Health.gov. "Nutrition and Health Are Closely Related." 2015.

42. Madden, Jenifer Joy. "How Walking Can Save America," Durable Human (blog), July 10, 2013.

43. National Cancer Institute. "Physical Activity and Cancer" fact sheet.

44. Centers for Disease Control. "Preventing Diabetes." CDC.gov.

45. Chan, Amanda. 2010. "Exercise Makes the Common Cold Less Common." LiveScience.com.

46. U.S. Department of Health and Human Services. 2015. "Step It Up! The Surgeon General's Call to Action to Promote Walking and Walkable Communities." Surgeongeneral.gov.

47. "People Who Exercise on Work Days Are Happier, Suffer Less Stress and Are More Productive." Daily Mail.com. December 16, 2008.

48. Ibid.

49. Malinowski, Melissa. Remarks. Bisnow Future of Office Event, Washington, D.C., March 24, 2015.

50. Griswold, Alison. 2012. "To Work Better, Just Get Up From Your Desk." Forbes. com. June 12, 2012.

51. U.S. Department of Health and Human Services. 2015. "Step It Up! The Surgeon General's Call to Action to Promote Walking and Walkable Communities." Surgeongeneral.gov.

52. Madden, Jenifer Joy. "How Walking Can Save America," Durable Human (blog), July 10, 2013.

53. Centers for Disease Control. Division of Nutrition, Physical Activity, and Obesity. "How Much Physical Activity Do Adults Need?" CDC.gov.

54. Bates, Daniel. 2013. "Ten Minutes of Exercise Is As Good As Hours in the Gym." Daily Mail.com, January 8, 2013.

55. Madden, Jenifer Joy. "Cubicle Dwellers: This Design's for You," Durable Human (blog), February 27, 2015.

56. Dunstan, D.W., et al. 2010. 'Too Much Sitting' and Metabolic Risk – Has Modern Technology Caught Up With Us? European Endocrinology 06(01).

57. Centers for Disease Control. 2015. "Prevalence of Obesity among Adults and Youth: United States, 2011–2014," NCHS Data Brief Number 219, November 2015.

58. Quinn, Fionnuala. "Bicycle Friendly Suburbs: The Push for Better Biking Beyond the Urban Core." American Bicyclist, Spring 2015. Bikeleague.org.

59. Dews, Fred. 2013. "Ninety Percent of Americans Drive to Work." Brookings Institution. Brookings.edu.

60. Jackson, Richard J. Remarks. Interview with the author. International Making Cities Livable Conference, Portland, Oregon, June 24, 2013.

61. Fenton, Mark. 2014. Youtube video. Posted by Durable Human. Live Healthy Fairfax Healthy Community Design Summit, Fairfax, Virginia, May 6, 2014.

62. Madden, Jenifer Joy. "How Walking Can Save America," Durable Human (blog), July 10, 2013.

63. Science Daily. "Do 'Walkable' Neighborhoods Reduce Obesity, Diabetes? Yes, Research Suggests." Science Daily, June 17, 2014.

64. National Association of Realtors. 2015. "Millennials Favor Walkable Communities, Says New NAR Poll," press release, July 28, 2015.

65. Speck, Jeff. 2013. *Walkable City: How Downtown Can Save America, One Step at a Time*, p. 50. New York City: Northpoint Press.

66. Phillips, Rick. Remarks. International Making Cities Livable Conference, Portland, Oregon, June 24, 2014.

67. Murphy, Liz. "Why Bike? It Makes Us Happy, Researchers Say." Bikeleague (blog), March, 16, 2015.

68. Newman, Peter. 2009. *Resilient Cities Responding to Climate Change*, p. 126. Washington, D.C.: Island Press.

69. Speck, Jeff. 2013. *Walkable City: How Downtown Can Save America, One Step At A Time*. New York City: Northpoint Press.

70. Madden, Jenifer Joy. "Portland, Oregon: Why Being Weird is Good for People," Durable Human (blog), July 16, 2014.

71. Ibid.

72. Stavenjord, Rebecca. Email to the author, March 24, 2015.

73. University of Illinois at Urbana-Champaign, Landscape and Human Health Laboratory. "Views of Greenery Help Girls Succeed." Lhhl.illinois.edu.

74. Kuo, Frances E. and Andrea Faber Taylor. 2004. A Potential Natural Treatment for Attention-Deficit/Hyperactivity Disorder: Evidence from a National Study. American Journal of Public Health 94(9).

75. Centers for Disease Control. "Number of Americans with Diabetes Projected To Double Or Triple by 2050," press release, October 22, 2010.

76. Louv, Richard. 2014. Remarks. George Washington University, Washington, D.C., March 14, 2014.

77. Centers for Disease Control and Prevention. Trends in the Prevalence of Extreme Obesity Among US Preschool-Aged Children Living in Low-Income Families, 1998-2010. Journal of the American Medical Association, 308(24): 2563-2565.

78. Egge, Rose. 2013. "Could Walking to School Reduce Childhood Obesity?" KomoNews.com.

79. National Center for Safe Routes to School. University of North Carolina Highway Safety Research Center. "At What Age Can Children Walk to School by Themselves?" Saferoutesinfo.org.

80. Harvard Medical School. 2004. Harvard Health Publications. "Calories burned in 30 minutes for people of three different weights." Health.harvard.edu.

81. Jackson, Richard. 2014. Interview with the author. International Making Cities Livable Conference, Portland, Oregon, June 24, 2014.

82. Di Noia, J. 2014. Defining Powerhouse Fruits and Vegetables: A Nutrient Density Approach. Prevention of Chronic Disease 11:130390.

83. U.S. Department of Health and Human Services and U.S. Department of Agriculture. December 2015. *2015–2020 Dietary Guidelines for Americans*. 8th Edition.

84. Centers for Disease Control. National Diabetes Prevention Program. 2015. "Prediabetes: Am I at Risk?"

85. Centers for Disease Control. National Diabetes Prevention Program. 2015. Infographic.

86. Morning Edition. 2015. "Fewer People Are Getting Diabetes, But the Epidemic Isn't Over." National Public Radio, December 4, 2015, reported by Nancy Shute.

87. American Academy of Pediatrics. "Kids and Vitamin D Deficiency," press release, October 18, 2012.

88. Vitamin D Deficiency and Rickets. 2015. HealthyChildren.org. November 21, 2015.

89. Loving, Robert D. 1980. Pediatrics. 66(3).

90. American Academy of Pediatrics. "Kids and Vitamin D Deficiency," press release, October 18, 2012.

91. National Institutes of Health. Office of Dietary Supplements. 2014. "Vitamin D Fact Sheet For Health Professionals."

92. Ibid.

93. Holick, Michael. 2004. Sunlight and Vitamin D for Bone Health and Prevention Of Autoimmune Diseases, Cancers, and Cardiovascular Disease. American Journal of Clinical Nutrition 80(6): 1678S-1688S.

94. American Academy of Dermatology. "Don't Seek the Sun." Pwrnewmedia.com. 2008.

95. Skin Cancer Foundation. "The D Dilemma." Skincancer.org.

96. Skin Flora. Wikipedia.

97. Morning Edition. 2013. "Getting Your Microbes Analyzed Raises Big Privacy Issues." National Public Radio, reported by Rob Stein. November 5, 2013.

98. Smithsonianmag.com. "The Healthy Truth about Traditional Childbirth." Video.

99. Morning Edition. 2013. "Getting Your Microbes Analyzed Raises Big Privacy Issues." National Public Radio, reported by Rob Stein. November 5, 2013.

100. Breindl, Anette. "Artificial Sweeteners Backfire Via Gut Microbiome." Bioworld.com. 2014.

101. Gilmore, Kat. 2015. Study Finds High-Fat Diet Changes Gut Microflora, Signals to Brain. UGA Today. Athens, Georgia: University of Georgia, July 7, 2015.

102. National Institutes of Health. 2013. Gut Microbes And Diet Interact To Affect Obesity. NIH Research Matters. September 16, 2013.

103. Smithsonianmag.com. 2013. "The Microbes We're Made of." Video.

104. Centers for Disease Control. 2015. "Antibiotic Resistance Questions and Answers." April 17, 2015.

105. Marshall, David. 2004. *Giants of Industry-Bill Gates*. Mason, Ohio: Blackbirch Press.

106. Bureau of Labor Statistics. 2013. "Time Use Survey." Bls.gov.

107. Wronski, Laura. Email to the author, November 22, 2013.

108. Steiner-Adair, Catherine. 2013. Remarks. Family Online Safety Institute, Washington, D.C., November 6, 2013.

109. Steiner-Adair, Catherine and Teresa H. Barker. 2013. *The Big Disconnect: Protecting Childhood And Family Relationships In The Digital Age.* New York: Harper Collins.

110. Morning Edition. 2014. "Orphans' Lonely Beginnings Reveal How Parents Shape a Child's Brain." National Public Radio, reported by Jon Hamilton, February 25, 2014.

111. Carli, Vladimir, et al. 2013. A Newly Identified Group of Adolescents at "Invisible" Risk for Psychopathology and Suicidal Behaviour: Findings from the SEYLE Study. World Psychiatry 13(1), February 4, 2014.

112. United Press International. Some Teens in South Korea Exhibiting 'Digital Dementia.' June 26, 2013.

113. Bronson, Po, and Ashley Merryman. 2009. *Nurture Shock: New Thinking about Children*. New York: Hachette Book Group.

114. Patchin, Justin. Remarks. Family Online Safety Institute Annual Conference, Washington, D.C., November, 2013.

115. Badger, Emily. 2013. "The Most Powerful Thing We Could Give Poor Kids Is Completely Free." Washington Post. November 3, 2015.

116. Turkle, Sherry. Remarks. Family Online Safety Institute, Washington, D.C., October 19, 2015.

117. Lewis, C.S. 2001. *Mere Christianity*. Grand Rapids, Mich.: Zondervan.

118. Davidson, Richard. Presentation. Mindfulness Leadership Summit, Washington, D.C., November 6, 2015.

119. The Diane Rehm Show. "New Research on Teens, Toddlers and Mobile Devices." November 5, 2015.

120. Ibid.

121. Madden, Jenifer Joy. "Kids Need Parents to Pay Attention," Durable Human (blog), January 3, 2014.

122. The Diane Rehm Show. "New Research on Teens, Toddlers and Mobile Devices." November 5, 2015.

123. Pew Research Center. January 7, 2016. Parents, Teens and Digital Monitoring.

124. Madden, Jenifer Joy. "Meet the First Middle School Community Organizers," Durable Human (blog), November 19, 2014.

125. Alexander, Jessica. 2015. "The Secret to Danish Happiness." Huffington Post. October 28, 2015.

126. Underwood, Emily. 2013. "Sleep: The Ultimate Brainwasher." Sciencemag.org. October 17, 2013.

127. Lulu, Xie, et al. 2013. Sleep Drives Metabolite Clearance from The Adult Brain. Science 342(6156):373-377.

128. National Institutes of Health. Research Matters. 2013. "How Sleep Clears the Brain." October 28, 2013.

129. Strand, Clark. 2015. *Waking Up to the Dark: Ancient Wisdom For a Sleepless Age*. New York: Spiegel & Grau.

130. The Kojo Nnamdi Show. "The Science of Sleep." Reported by Rebecca Sheir. August 18, 2014.

131. Gordon, Amie M. and Serena Chen. 2013. The Role of Sleep in Interpersonal Conflict: Do Sleepless Nights Mean Worse Fights? Social Psychological and Personality Science 5(2): 168-175.

132. Rosenberg, Jessica, et al. 2014. "Early to Bed, Early to Rise": Diffusion Tensor Imaging Identifies Chronotype-Specificity. NeuroImage 84(1): 428–434.

133. Prather, Aric A., et al. 2015. Behaviorally Assessed Sleep and Susceptibility to the Common Cold. Sleep. 38(9):1353–1359.

134. Pressler, Margaret Webb. 2012. "Aging Healthfully is Not Just a Matter of Having Good Genes." Washington Post, December 11, 2012.

135. Morning Edition. 2013. "Healthful Habits Can Help Induce Sleep Without the Pills." National Public Radio. Reported by Patti Neighmond. December 16, 2013.

136. Yetish, Gandhi, et al. 2015. Natural Sleep and Its Seasonal Variations in Three Pre-Industrial Societies. Current Biology 25(21) 2862–2868.

137. LeBlond, Lawrence. 2012. "Want a Good Night Sleep? Leave the Backlit Tablet out of the Bedroom." Redorbit.com. August, 20, 2012.

138. The Diane Rehm Show. 2014. "Brainstorm: The Power and Purpose of the Teenage Brain." January 6, 2014.

139. The Kojo Nnamdi Show. 2014. "The Science of Sleep." Reported by Rebecca Sheir. August 18, 2014.

140. Madden, Jenifer Joy. "3 Reasons To Use an Alarm Clock Instead of Your Phone," Durable Human (blog), April 16, 2015.

141. Palfrey, John, and Urs Gasser. 2008. *Born Digital: Understanding the First Generation of Digital Natives*. New York: Basic Books.

142. Commonsensemedia.org. 2015. "The Common Sense Consensus: Media Use by Tweens and Teens."

143. Internet Keep Safe Coalition (iKeepSafe). November 2015. "Cyberbalance in a Digital Culture."

144. Schnabel, Jim. 2012. "Your Memories Need Their Sleep," The Dana Foundation, August 7, 2012.

145. Kelly, Yvonne, John Kelly, and Amanda Sacker. 2013. Changes in Bedtime Schedules and Behavioral Difficulties in 7 Year Old Children. Pediatrics 132(5).

146. National Sleep Foundation. "Children and Sleep." Sleepfoundation.org.

147. National Sleep Foundation. "Teens and Sleep." Sleepfoundation.org.

148. Richtel, Matt. 2010. "Attached to Technology and Paying a Price." New York Times, June 7, 2010.

149. Council on Communications and Media. 2011. Media Use by Children Younger Than 2 Years. Pediatrics. 128(5).

150. Falbe, Jennifer, et al. 2015. Sleep Duration, Restfulness, Screens in the Sleep Environment. Pediatrics 135(2).

151. American Academy of Pediatrics. Council on Communications and Media. 2013. "Children, Adolescents, and the Media," policy statement. Pediatrics 132(5).

152. Spain, Erin. 2012. "Diagnosis of ADHD on the Rise." Northwestern University News. March 19, 2012.

153. Ellison, Katherine. 2012. "Pay More Attention to ADHD." The Washington Post, April 1, 2012.

154. American Academy of Pediatrics. "Go to Bed! Study Finds Irregular Bedtimes Linked to Behavior Problems in Children," press release, October 14, 2013.

155. National Sleep Foundation. "Children and Sleep." Sleepfoundation.org.

156. Buczynski, Ruth. 2015. Mindfulness Series, National Institute for the Clinical Application of Behavioral Medicine, November 23, 2015.

157. National Institutes of Health. National Institute on Deafness and Other Communication Disorders. Webpage. "Noise-induced Hearing Loss."

158. CBS News. 2010. "Teen Hearing Loss Rising." Video. CBSNews.com.

159. Shargorodsky, J., et al. 2010. Change in Prevalence of Hearing Loss in U.S. Adolescents. JAMA 304(7).

160. Brigham and Women's Hospital. 2010. "Hearing Loss in U.S. Teens Increased in Prevalence in the Previous 15 Years," press release.

161. Australian Hearing. 2013. "Is Australia Listening? Attitudes in Hearing Loss." Hearing.com.au.

162. Seliger, Susan. 2012. "Why Won't They Get Hearing Aids?" New York Times, April 5, 2012.

163. Mayo Clinic. "How You Hear." Slide show. Mayoclinic.com.

164. National Institutes of Health. Research Portfolio Online Reporting Tools. "Hair Cell Regeneration and Hearing Loss." Report.nih.gov.

165. National Institutes of Health. National Institute on Deafness and Other Communication Disorders. "Noise-induced Hearing Loss." Nidcd.nih.gov.

166. Occupational Safety & Health Administration. 2002. "Hearing Conservation." OSHA 3074.

167. National Institutes of Health. It's A Noisy Planet. "How Loud Is Too Loud? How Long Is Too Long?" Noisyplanet.nidcd.nih.gov.

168. American Automobile Association (AAA). Digest of Motor Laws. Drivinglaws. aaa.com/tag/headsets/.

169. Scholastic. "All About Blocks." Scholastic.com.

170. Madden, Jenifer Joy. "Games Are the Future – E. O. Wilson," Durable Human (blog), September 1, 2009.

171. American Optometric Association. "Computer Vision Syndrome." Aoa.org.

172. Vasudevan, Balamurali and Kenneth Ciufreda. 2006. "Nearwork-Induced Transient Myopia Following Interrupted Reading." Presentation. American Academy of Optometry Conference, Denver, Colorado, 2006.

173. Layton, Julia. 2008. "How Does the Body Make Electricity—And How Does It Use It?" Science.HowStuffWorks.com.

174. Ibid.

175. Apple. iPhone 4 Product Guide.

176. Reardon, Marguerite. 2011. "Cell Phone Radiation: A Self-Defense Guide (FAQ)." CNET.com.

177. Environmental Health Trust. "Cellphone Warnings." Ehtrust.org.

178. National Cancer Institute. "Cell Phones and Cancer Risk." Cancer.gov.

179. American Cancer Society. "Cellular Phones." Cancer.org.

180. World Health Organization. International Agency for Research on Cancer (IARC). 2011. "IARC Classifies Radiofrequency Electromagnetic Fields A Possibly Carcinogenic to Humans," press release, May 31, 2011.

181. MobilizeMovie.com. "Dan Brown, 50." Youtube video. Posted by Kevin Kunze, March 15, 2012.

182. MobilizeMovie.com. "Rich Farver, 28." Youtube video. Posted by Kevin Kunze, March 15, 2012.

183. Burrell, Lloyd. 2013. "Cell Phone Radiation Breast Cancer Link - New Study Raises Grave Concerns." NaturalNews.com, November 27, 2013.

184. American Cancer Society. 2011. "Breast Cancer Facts and Figures 2011-2012." Atlanta: American Cancer Society.

185. West, John G., et al. 2013. Case Report: Multifocal Breast Cancer in Young Women with Prolonged Contact Between Their Breasts and Their Cellular Phones. Case Reports in Medicine. August 19, 2013.

186. CBS News. 2015. "Cellphone Safety: Where Do You Keep Your Phone?" Reported by Elizabeth Hinson.

187. WTVR. November 19, 2012. "Doctors Question Link Between Breast Cancer and Where Women Keep Their Phones."

188. Ibid.

189. Federal Communications Commission. 2015. "Specific Absorption Rate (SAR) for Cell Phones: What It Means for You."

190. La Vignera, S., et al. Effects of the Exposure to Mobile Phones on Male Reproduction: A Review of the Literature. Journal of Andrology 33(3): 350-6. 2012.

191. Agarwal, A., et al. 2009. Effects of Radiofrequency Electromagnetic Waves (RF-EMW) from Cellular Phones on Human Ejaculated Semen: An In Vitro Pilot Study. Fertility and Sterility. 92(4): 1318-25.

192. Apple. Website. http://www.apple.com/legal/rfexposure/watch1,2/en/.

193. Malik, Ajay. 2015. "Why the FCC's Safety Guidelines for Wi-Fi Need To Be Re-Evaluated." Network World.com.

194. Ibid.

195. "EWG's Guide to Safer Cell Phone Use: 5 Safety Tips for Cellphone Use." Environmental Working Group, August 27, 2013. EWG.org.

196. "Cell Phone Use In Pregnancy May Cause Behavioral Disorders In Offspring." 2012. Yale School of Medicine. Scientific Reports 2:312, March 15, 2012.

197. Gardiner, Harry. Email to the author, January 5, 2016.

198. American Academy of Pediatrics. 2012. Letter to FCC Chair Genachowski from President Robert W. Block.

199. National Cancer Institute. 2013. "Cell Phones and Cancer Risk. What Do Expert Organizations Conclude?" Cancer.gov.

200. Schipper, David. 2015. "Do Cellphones Cause Cancer?" Consumer Reports, September 28, 2015.

201. Environmental Health Trust. "Environmental Health Trust Reveals Risky Patterns of Cell Phone Use by Middle Schoolers." Ehtrust.org.

202. Sherwin, Justin C., et al. 2011. Presentation. "The Association Between Time Spent Outdoors and Myopia in Children and Adolescents." 2011 American Academy of Ophthalmology Meeting, Orlando, Florida.

203. Davidson, Richard. 2015. Remarks. Mindful Leadership Summit, Washington, D.C., November 6, 2015.

204. Rosen, Larry. 2014. "ADHD and Technology: Helping Our Children Reclaim Their Focus and Attention," (blog). Huffington Post.com.

205. Cheadle, Harry. 2012. "What Is ASMR and Why Does It Make Me Feel So Good?" Vice.com, August 1, 2012.

206. Griswold, Alison. 2012. To Work Better, Just Get Up From Your Desk. Forbes, June 12, 2012.

207. Weil, Andrew. "Guided Meditation." Youtube video. Posted by thewilddivine, January 5, 2009.

208. Gordhamer, Soren. 2013. *Wisdom 2.0, The New Movement Toward Purposeful Engagement in Business and in Life.* New York: HarperCollins.

209. Huffington, Arianna. Remarks. Wisdom 2.0 Conference 2014. Youtube video posted by Wisdom 2.0, March 4, 2014.

210. Killingsworth, Matthew, and Daniel T. Gilbert. 2010. A Wandering Mind Is an Unhappy Mind. Science 330(6006) 932.

211. Goldstein, Elisha. 2012. "The STOP Practice." Youtube video, posted by NowEffect, January 11, 2012.

212. "Inner Explorer." Youtube video, posted by Wisdom 2.0, March 3, 2014.

213. Pickert, Kate. 2014. "The Mindful Revolution." TIME, January 23, 2014.

214. Nauert, Rick. 2010. "Meditation's Influence on Brain Activity." PsychCentral.com, March 26, 2010.

215. Siegel, Ronald D. "The Science of Mindfulness: A Research-Based Path to Well-Being." The Great Courses lecture series.

216. Kamarei, Golbie. 2015. Remarks. Mindful Leadership Summit, Washington, D.C., November 6, 2015.

217. Clay, Rebecca. 2001. Green Is Good for You. American Psychological Association 32(4).

218. Hoober, Steven, and Eric Berkman. 2011. *Designing Mobile Interfaces.* Sebastopol, Cal.: O'Reilly Media.

219. Pennebaker, Ruth. 2009. "The Mediocre Multitasker." New York Times, August 30, 2009.

220. Richtel, Matt. 2010. "Attached to Technology and Paying a Price." New York Times, June 7, 2010.

221. Gingerich, Amanda C. and Tara T. Lineweaver. 2014. OMG! Texting in Class = U fail :(Empirical Evidence That Text Messaging During Class Disrupts Comprehension. Teaching of Psychology 41(1) 44-51.

222. Weekend Edition Saturday. "Survey Finds Teens Spend Wealth of Time With Screens." National Public Radio, November 9, 2015, reported by Scott Simon.

223. Chen, Fang, et al. 2011. Multimodal Behavior and Interaction As Indicators of Cognitive Load. ACM Transactions on Interactive Intelligent Systems. Nicta.com.au.

224. Ibid.

225. Wikipedia. Sterile Cockpit Rule.

226. Hoober, Steven. 2012. "Eyes on the Road or Mind on the Road?" UxMatters.com, April 2, 2012.

227. Hoober, Steven. Email to the author. December 29, 2015.

228. Anderson, Chris. 2011. "How to Stop E-Mail Overload? Think Before You Hit Send." Washington Post, September 9, 2011.

229. Fiore, Faye. 2011. Our Twisted Relationship with the GPS. Los Angeles Times, February 8, 2011.

230. NBC News. "GPS Addict? It May Be Eroding Your Brain," reported by Joan Raymond, November 15, 2010.

231. Konishi, Kyoko and Véronique D. Bohbot. 2013. Spatial Navigational Strategies Correlate With Gray Matter in The Hippocampus of Healthy Older Adults Tested in a Virtual Maze. Frontiers in Aging Neuroscience. February 20, 2013.

232. Vebo Solutions. Website. Vebosolutions.com.

READ THE BOOK THAT LAUNCHED THE DURABLE HUMAN MOVEMENT!

Get your free digital copy today at
DurableHuman.com/FreeManifesto

Also available in paperback from Amazon and other booksellers.

And don't miss *The Durable Human Manifesto* read by the author and enhanced with music, giggling kids, and other sounds of life!

NOW AVAILABLE ON AUDIBLE AND iTUNES

About the author

JENIFER JOY MADDEN has informed the world about health and well-being on news outlets from ABC News to The Discovery Health Channel; *The Huffington Post* to *The Washington Post*; to her website, DurableHuman.com.

A member of the National Association of Science Writers and Society of Environmental Journalists, Jenifer is a multi-media reporter, design ethicist, digital communications professor, and award-winning community leader. But her most prized accomplishment is raising three loving, contributing, durable humans.